MASTERING METRICS

Official Module Guide

2nd edition

The Chartered Institute of Marketing
Moor Hall
Cookham
Maidenhead
Berkshire
SL6 9QH
United Kingdom

www.cim.co.uk

First published 2014

Revised edition published 2017
Second edition 2017

A catalogue record for this book is available from the British Library.

ISBN 978-1-907368-53-0 (paperback)
ISBN 978-1-907368-54-7 (ebook)

CONTENTS

1

3

INTRODUCTION

MARKETING IS CONSTANTLY EVOLVING AND IT'S IMPORTANT TO DEMONSTRATE YOU HAVE KEPT UP TO DATE WITH THE LATEST DEVELOPMENTS.

Following extensive research among marketing professionals and the wider business community we launched a portfolio of award-based qualifications to reflect the market need for flexible bite-sized learning for today's professional marketer.

Each individual module can be achieved as a distinct self-contained award and, when combined with further awards, built into a full qualification if and when required.

Each module is based on our unique Professional Marketing Standards, which are designed to help meet the ever-increasing demands on marketers at every stage of their career.

ABOUT US

CIM (The Chartered Institute of Marketing) is the leading international professional marketing body. CIM exists to develop the marketing profession, maintain professional standards and improve the skills of marketing practitioners, enabling them to deliver exceptional results for their organisations.

Our range of professional qualifications and training programmes – along with our extensive membership benefits – are all designed to support you, develop your knowledge, enable you to grow, and increase your network. Our professional pathway will help you excel and realise your full potential.

PROFESSIONAL MARKETING COMPETENCIES

The Professional Marketing Competencies are a framework that provide a guide to the skills and behaviours that are expected of professional marketers at varying levels of proficiency.

Developed from extensive research with employers and employees in marketing and other business functions, the Competencies give individuals and organisations the basis on which to assess the abilities of a capable and competent marketer.

More information about the Professional Marketing Competencies can be found on our website: www.cim.co.uk/competencies.

THE PROFESSIONAL MARKETING COMPETENCIES

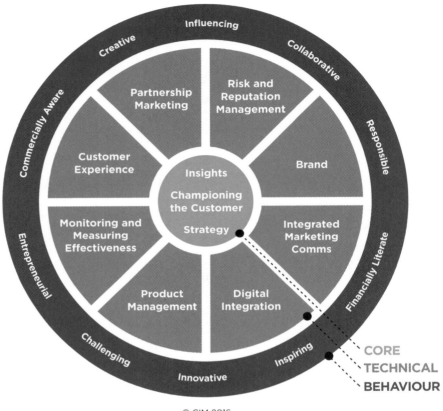

© CIM 2016

QUALIFICATION OVERVIEW

The Diploma in Professional Marketing gives you the required knowledge, skills and understanding at management level to enable you to take a strategic approach to marketing planning. By understanding key marketing metrics and measurement techniques you will be able to interpret relevant insight and make informed strategic decisions.

INTRODUCTION TO THE MODULE

Mastering Metrics is a mandatory module that sits within the suite of Diploma modules. To gain the CIM Diploma in Professional Marketing you need to pass this and the Strategic Marketing mandatory module, plus one elective module – either Driving Innovation or Digital Strategy. However, you will gain a module award for each individual module you pass.

MODULE CONTENT

This module examines the importance of managing marketing data in order to make effective marketing decisions. It explains the role of marketing metrics within the organisation and establishes how understanding a range of measurement techniques can enable the marketer to create marketing insights to support and inform strategic decision-making. It provides an appreciation of how measurement techniques, aligned to business objectives, can help to identify the most appropriate marketing activities for any situation, and gauge their effectiveness. It outlines the value of using appropriate data sources to enable effective marketing analysis, and of employing the most relevant analytics tools and techniques. The module also gives the marketer the ability to selectively analyse different sets of marketing data to uncover insights, and to optimise the use of marketing resources.

BENEFITS OF STUDYING THE MODULE

Being able to use a range of different marketing metrics allows the marketer to overcome one of the main challenges facing the discipline, function and profession of marketing – its perceived lack of accountability. Traditionally marketing has been one of the least measurable functions within organisations, despite its contribution to organisational success. But it is increasingly being called on to demonstrate its effectiveness, and the growing number of tools and techniques available to measure marketing activities are helping it to do this. The concepts covered in this module will help you to understand how to measure marketing, provide justification for the activities you carry out and inform decisions on future objectives and strategies. This will help you, as a professional marketer, to promote understanding throughout the organisation of the role marketing can play in success, building credibility for you and for marketing as a whole.

LEARNING OUTCOMES

The three units and six learning outcomes for this module are as follows:

1. Metrics and analytics:
- Understand the role of marketing metrics.
- Assess appropriate sources of reliable and robust data for marketing analytics.

2. Measuring effectiveness:
- Understand the significance of different measurement techniques across a range of market contexts.
- Determine the relevant measures of marketing performance for a range of organisations.

3. Analytics for decision-making:
- Interpret marketing metrics to establish the effectiveness of marketing activities
- Apply various analytics tools and techniques for marketing insight to support strategic decision-making.

PLAN YOUR JOURNEY

This study guide has been written to include all the syllabus indicative content from the Mastering Metrics unit.

Rather than basing the chapters directly on the syllabus learning outcomes and indicative content, categories of metrics have been amalgamated to link together the areas of commonality from the syllabus. This reduces repetition within the text, enabling you to more easily find and understand information covering all aspects of a particular area of marketing metrics.

We've included a glossary of metrics at the back. This clarifies the main text and avoids the need to repeat the technical description each time a metric is mentioned in the body of the text.

ASSESSMENTS

A variety of assessment methodologies are used for the Diploma in Professional Marketing, depending on the module you are studying. Assessment methods are employer driven, practitioner based, relevant and appropriate for business needs. In addition, the assessments for all qualifications comply with regulatory requirements, are fit for purpose, fair, valid, reliable and manageable, all of which creates confidence in the standard learners achieve.

The assessment methodology for this module is an assignment, which will be available to candidates six months before the deadline for completing and submitting it. Please refer to the module specifications on the website for more detail.

OTHER RESOURCES

This study guide is one aspect of a wide range of study resources available to you in the module toolkit. No single resource is sufficient to gain a full understanding of the module content. The study guide is intended to be used in conjunction with the core textbook, but you will also find it valuable to refer to the supplementary textbooks mentioned within the guide.

Recommended textbook
Farris, P.W., Bendle, N.T., Pfeifer, P.E. and Reibstein, D.J. (2017) *Key marketing metrics: the 50+ metrics every manager needs to know.* 2nd ed. Harlow, Pearson.

Further reading

Davis, J.A. (2013) *Measuring marketing: 110+ key metrics every marketer needs.* 2nd edition. Chichester, John Wiley.

Farris, P.W., Bendle, N.T., Pfeifer, P.E. and Reibstein, D.J. (2015) *Marketing metrics: the definitive guide to measuring marketing performance.* 3rd ed. New Jersey, Pearson. [This is the same as the recommended test but US edition – and is available as a Kindle version.]

Hemann, C. and Burbary, K. (2013) *Digital marketing analytics: making sense of consumer data in a digital world.* Indianapolis, QUE.

Marr, B. (2015) *Big data: using smart big data, analytics and metrics to make better decisions and improve performance.* Chichester, John Wiley & Sons.

Marr, B. (2016) *Big data in practice: how successful companies use big data analytics to deliver extraordinary results.* Chichester, John Wiley & Sons.

McDonald, M., Mouncey, P and Maklan, S. (2014) *Marketing value metrics.* 2nd ed. London, Kogan Page.

The textbooks cover the topics in this module in much more detail than this study guide – but they have not been written with the CIM's syllabus in mind. To enable you to extend your knowledge, the study guide also summarises ideas and concepts from a range of key sources, many of which are available via the CIM's study website. It is always a good idea to read the original papers because they usually provide insights into a theory or case study that a brief summary is unable to do. So, the study guide provides you with an overview of the content of the module and acts as a bridge to further resources.The study guide also provides you with a range of short case studies and practical exercises to help you put some of the theories and frameworks into context. In preparing the assignment for this module's assessment you will need to apply a range of concepts and tools to a real organisation – so the exercises here will give you some practice. Finally, each chapter contains a short quiz to help you consolidate your learning.

MyCIM

CIM itself offers a variety of resources to all its members, including Study Resources, Marketing Expert, Content Hub, MyiLibrary, Ebsco and Emerald. You can find these at www.cim.co.uk within MyCIM.

My Study Resources

These are guides to help you delve deeper into material that supports the six learning outcomes in this module. The links are taken from a range of resources and direct you to the wide range of online member resources to help your learning journey.

Marketing Expert and Content Hub

Marketing Expert has a range of practical guides, templates, topic guides and legal notes on marketing. Content Hub has blogs, editorials, podcasts, webinars on a range of marketing topics.

MyiLibrary

The library at Moor Hall is open to all learners Monday to Friday between the hours of 9am and 5pm. For those who can't get to it, MyiLibrary is a good alternative. It allows you to read a range of marketing books on your desktop, and, in some cases, you can download them to your e-reader for seven days.

Ebsco and Emerald

Ebsco is an online database of reference material that is updated every day. It includes journals, magazines, newspapers and reports covering all aspects of marketing and business from around the world. Learners also have full access to the Emerald marketing eJournal collection. An online user guide provides a detailed list of current titles and information on how to search the collection. It also contains a range of older editions that the library has subscribed to historically.

Remember, all of this information is available via MyCIM.

Finally, one further way you can develop your knowledge and understanding is to keep up to date with what's going on in the real world of marketing. All members can access *Catalyst*, our magazine, free, but magazines such as *Campaign*, *Marketing Week* and *The Drum* provide a wealth of informative, insightful and fascinating information, augmented by up-to-date opinion, blogs, stories and resources on their websites. You could also follow the hundreds of publishers, marketing theorists, academics, companies, brands and agencies who post content on social media.

Or you could take advantage of Cutting Edge, the CIM's weekly digest of short and snappy marketing-related news items from across the sectors, available at www.cim.co.uk/cuttingedge when logged into MyCIM.

Please note: All information included in this Introduction was correct at the time of going to print. Please check the Study Connect e-newsletters for any updates or changes.

1.0
THE ROLE OF MARKETING METRICS

OUTLINE

This chapter explains why it is so important for marketers to measure performance and to understand the link between business goals, strategy and marketing metrics. At the end of this chapter you will be able to:

- Understand why marketing metrics are important.
- Understand the 'triple bottom line' of people, planet and profit.
- Understand the range of metrics.
- Recognise the growing trend towards integrated reporting.
- Recognise the working practices and processes needed to enhance the implementation and use of metrics.
- Understand the risk to an organisation if performance related metrics not implemented.
- Understand the importance of engaging with stakeholders.

THE ORGANISATIONAL CONTEXT FOR MARKETING METRICS

Marketing metrics have become increasingly important for a number of reasons. Perhaps most important among them is the growing need for marketing to demonstrate the value it adds to the business, and marketers are, therefore, increasingly being held to account for their activities. Resources are scarce, and the belt-tightening that was required during the recession has now become 'business as usual'. To justify its spend and secure future budgets from the board, marketing has to speak the language of business – that is, finance – and back up its decisions with solid data and sound evidence. What's more, successful marketing (marketing that helps the business to achieve its strategic goals) depends on aligning everyone in the organisation behind a 'customer-first' orientation, and having clear analytics about the activities that deliver the greatest return helps to communicate to different functions why this is so important. It also reduces the potential for tension and conflict.

Also, the advance of digital technology means there is so much more data available these days to facilitate measurement. The McKinsey Global Institute (2011) described the proliferation of data, including so-called 'big data', as follows: "The increasing volume and detail of information captured by enterprises, the rise of multimedia, social media, and the Internet of Things, will fuel exponential growth in data for the foreseeable future."

Marketing needs to measure its activity in order to answer fundamental business questions such as:

1. Are we achieving our goals?
2. How far are we from achieving them?
3. Are our activities working?
4. Where have we been and where are we now?
5. How can we improve?

ACTIVITY 1

Your own organisation may have additional reasons for analysing the success of your marketing strategies, tactics and programmes. List these reasons in order of importance and consider the implications for the organisation generally and the marketing function specifically if these activities weren't measured.

Sorger (2013) identifies five benefits of analysing marketing:

1. To drive revenue.
2. To save money.
3. To persuade executives.

4. To encourage experimentation.
5. To reduce internal politics.

Definitions

There are many terms used within the field of 'marketing metrics', and for clarity we list some definitions below.

Analytics and metrics – These two words are often used interchangeably, but they are different and we need to distinguish between them.

- **A metric** – Is 'a measuring system that quantifies a trend, dynamic or characteristic'. (Farris *et al* 2009) More generally, a metric is a measure of performance and, in the context of marketing, it is a measure of marketing performance.
- **An analytic** – In the current environment 'analytics' is most often associated with online activity, a trend reinforced by organisations' widespread use of Google Analytics to find and understand data about visitors to their websites. More broadly, analytics are tools used to provide data for metrics. In other words, analytics outputs are used as inputs for metrics.

Analytics are the tools and methods of analysis, while metrics are the results of the analysis and inform decision-making. So organisations need both. While we concentrate on metrics in this book, we also cover some of the sources of information – or analytical tools – needed to create these metrics.

Data and information – The words data, information, intelligence, knowledge and insight are also often used interchangeably, but here too it is important to distinguish between them.

If we imagine the words describing a sort of hierarchy, **data** – the raw output from metrics (numbers, words and pictures) – sits at the bottom. But data lacks context: on its own it doesn't tell us anything beyond the simple fact or facts it states. When various pieces of data are collected together, however, they start to have meaning and become information. When this **information** is manipulated and applied, it gives us **intelligence** (which is very close to **knowledge**) and this, in turn, provides **insights** into the ways consumers, markets and marketing work.

However, these definitions are not absolute – there are many shades of grey between one term and the next. The most important thing to remember is that metrics data in the form of numbers, pictures, graphs and so on are mere facts which, to be useful, we need to analyse, interpret, understand in context and, above all, complement with other data to provide a holistic understanding of the particular issue we are seeking to understand.

Aligning business objectives, strategies and metrics

According to Kotter (2013): "only 29% of ... employees can correctly identify their company's strategy [when given] six choices" – and other studies report even lower figures.

Every organisation needs clearly defined business objectives, and if these are communicated throughout the organisation, different functions, and individuals within those functions, can align their own goals with them, reducing the potential for internal conflict. The statistic from Kotter highlights how few employees are aligned with the organisation strategy, and he goes on to discuss the problems this can cause, stating that if employees "[don't] know what they are striving toward and [are] operating on false assumptions, [they] will move slowly and defensively rather than swiftly and proactively. Worst of all, they might be off and running, applying valuable energy in the wrong direction. With a clear understanding of the strategic priorities, people will move quickly to get you closer to those goals." So the strategy needs to be clearly explained and understood, and clear metrics aligned to the strategy will help employees to understand how they can implement what is expected of them.

Palmer *et al* (2007) cite Hastings (1996) in providing a hierarchical structure of mission and goals for an organisation (see Fig 1.1 below). Taking this structure as a base, you can develop and measure sub-goals and objectives.

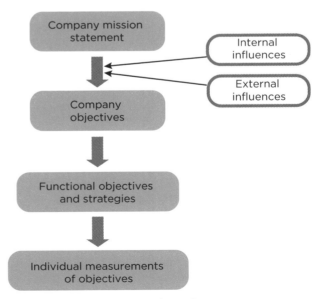

Fig 1.1 Hierarchy of mission and goals *(adapted)*

When attempting to gauge the success of the business strategy we need to use measures that are appropriate to what it is trying to achieve. As an example, you would use different measures of success if you were looking to enter a new market from those you would use when getting out of a market. When entering a new market, for example, you would look at sales, market growth, trends within the market, awareness, return on investment, competitive measures, profit, cost incurred and so on. When exiting a market, measures would include the level of investment made, the impact on other products or services, the costs of exit (penalty clauses, redundancies etc), asset depreciation and so on.

But with so many metrics to choose from, you have to ensure you select ones that are:

1. Most clearly linked and related to the objectives that you've set.
2. In keeping with how the organisation or specific functions within it measure the success of activities, strategies and objectives.

It's also important to ensure functional and individual goals are aligned with the overall objectives of the business. This gives employees a clear line of sight between what they do and the organisation's success, which helps to motivate them, keeps objectives on track and makes it easier to allocate roles and tasks. Clear communication is essential throughout to ensure that everyone in the organisation knows where it is heading and to help to integrate marketing activities with other functional activities so that they are all pulling in the same direction. By aligning all the objectives, from the vision and mission statement at the top of the hierarchy down to individual employee goals at the bottom, organisations maximise their chances of meeting their objectives.

Wilson and Gilligan (2009) establish guidelines for setting objectives. They suggest they should be:

1. **Hierarchical** – Start with the most important objective and rank the rest accordingly.
2. **Quantitative** – Ensure the objective is measurable.
3. **Realistic** – Base objectives on analysis rather than wishful thinking.
4. **Consistent** – Ensure all the objectives are aligned and pointing in the same direction.

CASE STUDY

The National Trust

The National Trust manages 300 historic properties in England, Wales and Northern Ireland, which are open to the public. But research showed that the general public perceived the Trust to be out of date, too formal ('Keep off the grass' was a phrase many associated with it) and appropriate only for certain demographic groups – particularly middle-class people over 50. The marketing team realised its stuffy image was deterring people from visiting the properties – let alone becoming members – so in 2011 it launched a campaign aimed at tackling its image problem and attracting new visitors. The central idea was to demonstrate that the National Trust was about far more than stately homes. The team wanted people to see it as a gateway to a wide variety of experiences for all ages, from hiking along stunning coastlines, to browsing in farm shops, to giving children the chance to run around in the countryside. As part of the Trust's 'Time Well Spent' campaign, which had been running for more than three years, the team wanted to reinforce the idea that the Trust provided an opportunity for "simple pleasures and quality, memorable experiences at affordable rates."

The campaign was designed to reach as many people as possible, with the aim of increasing the number of visitors and growing membership. A key performance indicator was whether people were considering a visit, so the Trust wanted to grow this measure too.

The budget for the campaign was just over £1 million, and this was allocated to different channels according to how effective these had proved for previous campaigns:

- 30% of the budget was allocated to outdoor advertising, including posters in railway and London Underground stations.
- 25% was set aside for press adverts, including broadsheet newspapers such as the Daily Telegraph, the Independent and the Daily Mail.
- 25% was earmarked for advertising on websites including Netmums, Weather.com, AOL's weather channel and ITV.com.
- 20% was reserved for radio.

Each advert used a slogan beginning with the words 'Time to...' followed by different messages, including 'be together', 'explore', 'unwind', 'see something new', 'visit your local' and 'feel free'.

In 2011, the number of people visiting National Trust properties increased by 16%, bringing the total number of individual visits to 17.7 million. Membership grew by 600,000 to four million. These were the highest volumes of visitors and members ever. In addition, nearly 10% of visitors were converted to members. Propensity to visit also grew: 82% of respondents said they would consider visiting a National Trust property in 2011, compared with 74% per cent in 2010, and 70% per cent of people surveyed said the campaign had improved their view of the brand too. The National Trust is continuing to follow this strategy, and it aims to have five million members by 2020.

Source: McMeeken, R., (2012) A fresh start. The Marketer, *February.*

The 'triple bottom line' and integrated reporting

The main driver in most commercial organisations is profit. But the growing emphasis on 'sustainability' (organisations will only be successful in the long term if they pay attention to all their stakeholders, not just their shareholders), and associated developments in reporting, mean that organisations (and marketers within them) can no longer afford to think about profits alone, but also about how those profits are made. Where organisations factor sustainability objectives into their strategies, metrics have to reflect these.

The triple bottom line (people, planet, profit) – There is a growing understanding that sustainable businesses have to put people (employees, customers, suppliers, communities etc) and the environment first. Without people and without natural resources, a company won't survive very long. The phrase 'triple bottom line' was first used in 1994 by John Elkington, a world authority on corporate responsibility and sustainable development. He argued that *only* by measuring its social, environmental and financial performance can an organisation take full account of the 'real' cost of doing business. Its 'people account', 'planet account' and 'profit account' are the three areas that make up its triple bottom line. Growing numbers of companies have espoused this thinking, and businesses including BT, Shell and AT&T have adopted triple-bottom-line reporting, not because they are altruistic, but because they know it makes good business sense.

By measuring the triple bottom line an organisation is, in effect, putting corporate social responsibility (CSR) at the centre of its activities. Companies that adopt this strategic approach to CSR avoid the charges of 'greenwashing' levelled at companies that appear to 'bolt on' CSR activities as little more than a PR exercise.

Investors understand the distinction too. Fourteen years ago Norman and MacDonald (2003) identified that the social and ethical attributes of an organisation were becoming increasingly important to shareholders when considering long-term investment decisions. The investment community's growing interest in companies practising triple-bottom-line reporting has been manifested in 30 conferences across the US, Asia and Europe over the past 15 years by just one conference company, TBLI Conference™. And there have been many similar conferences arranged by other organisations for the benefit of investors keen to develop portfolios of shares in organisations with triple-bottom-line credentials.

However, triple-bottom-line reporting is not easy for companies to do. *The Economist* (2009) reported some of the difficulties they face: "One problem with the triple bottom line is that the three separate accounts cannot easily be added up. It is difficult to measure the planet and people accounts in the same terms as profits – that is, in terms of cash. The full cost of an oil-tanker spillage, for example, is probably immeasurable in monetary terms, as is the cost of displacing whole communities to clear forests, or the cost of depriving children of their freedom to learn in order to make them work at a young age."

Such difficulties mean that companies that get involved in triple-bottom-line activities may still be criticised for 'greenwashing' – defined by the *Financial Times* as "the overstating of the environmentally- or socially-conscious attributes of a firm's offering and the understating of the negative attributes for the firm's benefit." The *FT* goes on to state that greenwashing can be both explicit and implicit, and be expressed in many forms, including promotional claims, labels or even the partnerships and relationships organisations get involved in.

Some examples it cites include the following:

- A chicken producer labels its products on store shelves as 'all natural' despite the fact the company treats its chickens with antibiotics.
- Plastic disposable water bottles are presented as 'eco-friendly' because they use less plastic than some other bottles.
- An oil company made much of its 'renewable energy' credentials in a rebranding exercise and associated television advertisements, but the *FT* calculated that only 0.25% of the company's energy is produced through 'alternative' sources.

Forbes magazine points out that an environmental stance is very difficult to fake – especially when your company is in an environmentally sensitive industry. Some companies have pursued a successful green agenda from the beginning. Outdoor clothing brand Patagonia is an example. One of its best-known initiatives was the 'buy less' campaign, which actively advised people not to buy what they didn't need. While this might seem at odds with the need to make profit, the idea of 'profitable good' embedded in its core business model has boosted its value proposition.

Many factors contribute to an organisation's triple bottom line, and these will vary depending on the organisation's context. Fig 1.2 indicates some areas to which metrics can be applied.

Environmental
- Reduce the 'footprint' that negatively impacts on environment
- Lower pollutants and emissions
- Reduce energy wastage
- Reduce usage of non-renewable energy
- Minimise climate change agents
- Use sustainable packaging, eg wood pulp from managed forests
- Recycle
- Source produce locally

Social
- CSR initiatives
- Fair trading
- Support local suppliers
- Reduce promotion of addictive substances and foods that contribute to obesity, and focus on healthier alternatives

Economic
- Ensure future economic development of company
- Create sustainable financial bottom line
- Minimise negative impact on other countries' economies
- Save money by reducing energy use

Fig 1.2 Measures in the triple bottom line *(Source: The Chartered Institute of Marketing, 2007)*

An organisation that adopts triple-bottom-line reporting has to:

- **Be accountable** – For its actions and approach to conducting business in the local and wider communities and within the organisation itself.
- **Be transparent** – In its dealings and decision-making, making data available where required.
- **Engage with stakeholders** – To build trust and relationships with different stakeholder groups.
- **Have integrated policies** – That take into account different perspectives when making strategic business decisions.
- **Adopt multi-layered reporting** – Through taking a balanced approach to measuring the success of its goals, objectives, strategies and tactics.

Integrated reporting (<IR>) – This moves beyond the triple bottom line to demonstrate how an organisation creates value in the widest sense. A relatively new method of reporting, it is already gaining currency among many organisations and institutions. The purpose of integrated reporting is to bring together information about an organisation's strategy, governance, performance and prospects in a way that reflects the commercial, social and environmental context it operates within.

The International Integrated Reporting Council (IIRC) has spearheaded the development and adoption of integrated reporting with the aim of creating an external reporting format to meet the complex and connected needs of today's stakeholders. In December 2013 it launched a framework for integrated reporting, which it defines as: "a process founded on integrated thinking that results in a periodic integrated report by an organisation about value creation over time and related communications regarding aspects of value creation. An integrated report is a concise communication about how an organisation's strategy, governance, performance and prospects, in the context of its external environment, lead to the creation of value in the short, medium and long term." (For further information, see http://www.theiirc.org/)

The triple bottom line and <IR> have similar principles at their core. The IIRC defines <IR> as a way to report "value creation for the organisation and for others," recognising that "value created by an organisation over time manifests itself in increases, decreases or transformations of the capitals caused by the organisation's business activities and outputs."

The IIRC goes on to state that the value an organisation creates has two inter-related aspects – the value created for the organisation and the value created for others:

*   **The organisation itself** – Financial returns to the providers of financial resources (as with the profit element of the triple bottom line).
*   **Others** – Including the stakeholders and society at large (related to the people and planet elements of the triple bottom line).

The Chartered Institute of Management Accountants (CIMA) has a key role in the IIRC, and provides valuable advice and information about the use and benefits of <IR>. It summarises benefits to investors, employees and other stakeholders as follows:

- **Investors** – Investors increasingly use non-financial factors as benchmarks for risk, recognising that financial performance and non-financial factors are linked. Integrated reporting provides a framework for an organisation to present a holistic picture of performance.
- **Employees** – Integrated reporting provides a framework to help organisations build engagement with employees and facilitate a two-way process for continual improvement.
- **Other stakeholders** – Many different stakeholders want to know about the factors affecting the performance of an organisation and its ability to create value over time. These stakeholders include customers, suppliers, business partners, local communities, regulators and policy makers. In countries whose economies are part of global company supply chains, governments are interested too.

The elements of an integrated report – According to the IIRC, an integrated report should include eight 'content elements', each answering a different question.

1. **Organisational overview and external environment** – What does the organisation do and what are the circumstances under which it operates?
2. **Governance** – How does the organisation's governance structure support its ability to create value in the short, medium and long term?
3. **Business model** – What is the organisation's business model?
4. **Risks and opportunities** – What are the specific risks and opportunities that affect the organisation's ability to create value over the short, medium and long term, and how is the organisation dealing with them?
5. **Strategy and resource allocation** – Where does the organisation want to go and how does it intend to get there?
6. **Performance** – To what extent has the organisation achieved its strategic objectives for the period and what are its outcomes in terms of effects on the capitals?
7. **Outlook** – What challenges and uncertainties is the organisation likely to encounter in pursuing its strategy, and what are the potential implications for its business model and future performance?
8. **Basis of presentation** – How does the organisation determine what matters to include in the integrated report and how are such matters quantified and evaluated?

1.2

THE MAJOR AREAS OF MARKETING METRICS

Accountants and marketers are starting to understand each other better: the former now have a greater appreciation of what marketing can deliver, while the latter are learning to speak the language of business – that is, finance. This is leading to, as well as being the result of, marketers and accountants working more closely together and greater integration of financial and marketing reporting. One manifestation of this is the greater acknowledgement by accountants of the importance of brands. Intangible assets, including brands, typically account for between 30% and 70% of a company's market value – a reversal of the situation 30 years ago. Organisations have long had to report the value of brands they have acquired on the balance sheet, though home-grown brands may not yet be reported. In turn, this places a large onus on marketers to demonstrate and quantify (using metrics) their brand-building capabilities. We discuss brand metrics in more detail below.

Key marketing-metric models – Defining key marketing metrics is not easy, not least because they tend to be organisation and lifecycle-stage specific. However, we can talk in terms of broad areas, and we explain these below.

A. MARKET AND BRAND METRICS

Markets are one of the most important areas for marketers to measure, because markets are the ultimate source of their revenue. A large part of the marketer's role is about creating competitive advantage, which encourages customers to use the products and services from their organisation rather than those of its competitors. Therefore, understanding actual and potential market share is an essential requirement. To gain this understanding they use market performance measures to help assess their company's market position in relation to its competitors, its customers and its overall performance.

Market metrics
Key measures of market performance are:

Market share – This is a measure of the organisation's sales as a percentage of the total sales volume in their industry, sector or market, or product area. Market share can be expressed in units or as a monetary value. For example, in unit terms Toyota had 3.91% of the UK car market by volume in 2013, selling 88,648 cars in a total market of 2,264,737 car sales. This represented an increase in volume for the company but a reduction in market share compared with 2012, because the whole market increased by a higher percentage. Companies use market share as a measure to help them gauge the success of their market penetration strategies, and they often use it as a target measure within objectives for future planning too. You can set market share targets by product or product line. HTC, for example, aims for a share of the market for smartphones with screens over 4.7 inches.

Relative market share – This is used to compare the organisation and its closest competitor. It helps marketers to understand how their organisation, or a particular product, is performing against the key competition. Because volume can affect both the market positioning an organisation adopts and the profits it expects to make, market share can be a vital measure to inform decisions on where to focus investment in brand building.

Market growth – This is determined by comparing sales in one year against those in the previous period. Knowing how fast a market is growing or shrinking is an important factor in understanding the organisation's competitive position. Let's take the Toyota example above. The company grew its sales in the UK in 2013 by 4,085 units – a 4.8% increase on the previous year, which would seem to be successful. But the market overall grew by 10.8%, so Toyota underperformed against the market in volume terms. Market growth rates help an organisation to understand market potential – with the proviso that growth rates may not continue as they have done previously. You also need to consider variables within market growth rates – notably whether the number of customers is growing, or if each customer is buying more of the product, or both. Fully understanding this measure helps marketers to predict for the future and determine strategies for the organisation.

Market penetration – This is related to market share. One of the four growth strategies proposed by Ansoff (1957) (and the least risky), increasing market penetration involves increasing sales to the existing market. To measure it you compare current sales against potential market demand for your products. Understanding the potential growth remaining helps marketers to make decisions about how to increase penetration. For example, if an organisation has high preference among existing customers but low awareness overall, it might decide to increase penetration through marketing tactics designed to increase awareness.

Brand metrics

Kotler et al (1999) described a brand as "a name, term, sign, symbol or design, or a combination of these, that identifies the goods or services of one seller or group of sellers and differentiates them from the competition."

McDonald and Wilson (2011), define a brand similarly, as "a name or symbol which identifies a product. A successful brand identifies a product as having a sustainable, competitive advantage."

Brand metrics can help to provide marketers with an understanding of the complexities of brand valuation, while enabling non-marketers to gain an appreciation of the factors that can drive brand value.

Key brand measures are as follows:

Brand equity – Through developing competitive advantage and customer preference, marketers can create not just a return on investment from marketing activities but also an increase in value for the total organisation. This value is the 'brand equity', and it can apply equally to individual products and the organisation as a whole. It is the value that drives competitive advantage, so it is essential to measure it. There is no single approach to measuring brand equity, however, as it involves measuring intangible elements that can be difficult to define. Even the specialist brand valuation consultancies, such as Interbrand and Brand Finance, measure brand value in different ways. Such companies produce annual lists of brands, ranked by value, based on their respective proprietary methodologies. Fig 1.3, which shows the most recent top ten global brands lists from three of the leading valuation companies, shows just how subjective brand valuation and brand equity is. Interbrand values Apple at $178 billion, Brand Finance values it at $107 billion and Millward Brown's BrandZ at $235 billion.

	Brand value league tables					
	Interbrand $m (2016)		Brand Finance $m (2017)		BrandZ (2017)	
1	Apple	178,119	Google	109,470	Google	245,581
2	Google	133,252	Apple	107,141	Apple	234,671
3	Coca-Cola	73,102	Amazon	106,396	Microsoft	143,222
4	Microsoft	72,102	AT&T	87,016	Amazon	139,286
5	Toyota	53,580	Microsoft	76,265	Facebook	129,800
6	IBM	52,500	Samsung	66,219	AT&T	115,112
7	Samsung	51,808	Verizon	65,875	VISA	110,999
8	Amazon	50,338	Walmart	62,211	Tencent	108,292
9	Mercedes-Benz	43,490	Facebook	61,998	IBM	102,088
10	GE	43,130	ICBC	47,832	McDonald's	97,323

Fig 1.3 Comparison of three brand league tables *(Sources: Interbrand, Brand Finance and Millward Brown – BrandZ)*

For many years Interbrand ranked Coca-Cola as the world's most valuable brand, but digital brands are rising rapidly through the ranks. Brand equity considerations need to be a factor in all marketing decisions, given that much of the purpose of marketing is to increase the value of the organisational and product/service brands.

Brand image/position – This is measured as the customers' perception of the brand compared with competitors. Understanding the customers' view of the brand is obviously important when considering changes to the product or brand proposition.

Brand premium – When a product is clearly distinctive and superior to its competitors, it offers clear value to the customer. In such circumstances you can adopt a premium pricing strategy. Apple, for example, makes distinctive products and there are customers who value this distinctiveness sufficiently to pay far more for an Apple product than they would for an equivalent product from a competitor. Because the potential brand premium is key to the pricing strategy, developing strategies to increase the brand premium is often central to marketing planning.

B. CUSTOMER PROFILING, SATISFACTION AND LOYALTY METRICS

If a key role of marketing is to develop competitive advantage to encourage customers to use the products and services of one organisation as opposed to those of another, it is clearly important to understand those customers fully. The main areas the marketer has to consider are the **needs of customers** and how to **segment the market** into customer groups.

Customer needs can be identified as:

- **Articulated** – Those things the customer asks for clearly and directly – for example, "I would like these trousers but do you have them in blue rather than black?"
- **Latent** – The needs that the customer has but that are largely hidden or unknown. Henry Ford, head of the eponymous Ford Motor Company, famously said that had he asked his customers what they wanted they would have said 'a faster horse'.

Marketing is about meeting existing needs, but also about identifying the needs that customers have but sometimes aren't even aware of, and this is where innovation and invention come in.

Understanding customer needs, whether articulated or latent, enables an organisation to increase its appeal to particular customer groups, or 'target segments'.

There are many different definitions of segmentation and what constitutes a segment. McDonald (2004) defines segmentation as: "Groups of individuals, or organisations, who have the same or similar needs which will be satisfied by the same or similar offers." Segments are, he says:

- Identifiable and recognisable (by the members of the segment).
- Exist independently (if your organisation didn't exist, the segment would still be there).
- Measurable (even if it's difficult).
- Substantial (big enough to be worth investing in).
- Externally accessible and actionable (for example, you can promote to them through channels).

McDonald and Mouncey (2009) suggest that metrics for measuring customer segments can be divided into two categories:

1. Those that define and track the segment over time (and that are independent of the organisation):
   - Needs and wants.
   - Attitudes and opinions.
   - Demographic.
   - Geographic.
   - Geodemographic.
   - Psychographic.
   - Media consumption.
2. Those relating to the performance and goals of the segment itself:
   - Market share.
   - Sales volumes.
   - Gross margin.
   - Brand image.
   - Customer value.

The most important metrics for measuring customer satisfaction, customer service and loyalty are as follows:

Customer satisfaction – This is generally based on survey data and is expressed as a rating, often a simple percentage approval rating – for example, a satisfaction rating of 83%. Customer satisfaction is a key measure within many organisations as it helps to focus employees' attention on the importance of meeting customers' needs. Falling satisfaction levels are indicators of problems that will affect sales and profitability. Customer satisfaction is a major objective of most marketing teams, because without satisfied customers the organisation will not survive.

Willingness to recommend – When a customer is highly satisfied with a product/service or an organisation they may be willing to recommend it to others. This gives an organisation a big marketing advantage as word of mouth is one of the most powerful communication tools available. It is also free. Social media has made word of mouth/ willingness to recommend even more important because rather than just recommending to friends, relations, colleagues and others, social media allows people to communicate much more widely. The downside, of course, is that negative comments can spread like wildfire too.

Net Promoter Score® (NPS®) – This is a customer loyalty metric developed in 2003 by management consultant Frederick Reichheld of Bain and Company, in collaboration with the company Satmetrix. It assesses to what extent someone would recommend a certain company, product or service to his or her friends, relatives or colleagues, using a scale of 0-10. The results allow companies to divide customers into three groups:

- **Promoters** – Those willing to recommend the organisation (rating of 9 or 10).
- **Passives** – Satisfied but unenthusiastic (rating of 7 or 8).
- **Detractors** – Unwilling to recommend the organisation (rating of 0 to 6).

A high net promoter score indicates the organisation is doing well in terms of customer satisfaction.

Retention rate – Marketers need to retain customers as well as attract them, particularly as it is almost always cheaper to keep an existing customer than it is to acquire a new one. The retention rate is used to measure the percentage of the organisation's customers that it retains over a given time period. Customer retention is a key objective of many organisations, because a lost customer means not only lost sales but also loss of the investment incurred in attracting them in the first place. Because high customer retention is desirable marketers need to develop strategies to improve the retention rates.

Churn rates – 'Churn', or 'attrition', is the rate at which a company loses customers. Inevitably some customers will leave, for a variety of reasons, but understanding how many customers are moving on each year and what the trends are is important. Mobile phone operators experience high churn rates for example, as customers switch providers in search of more attractive deals. The number of customers per operator stays relatively stable, but those customers will be different every year: the sector (in the UK) has a typical churn rate of nearly 10%.

ACTIVITY 4

Calculate the retention and churn rates for your organisation for the past two years to see if the metrics have improved. If possible, compare them to those of your competitors in order to evaluate your organisation's performance within the sector.

C. CHANNEL AND DISTRIBUTION METRICS

Channel or 'place' considerations relate to understanding where and how customers buy products. Location is only a small part of this, and is arguably increasingly less important as more and more transactions take place online. Growing numbers of organisations are using specialist intermediaries in order to ensure that stock is readily available and can be delivered to customers in a timely way (a process known as 'fulfilment'), while others use their own controlled outlets – Apple stores being an obvious example. The organisation should therefore have metrics that cover these areas in addition to specific measures for the efficiency and effectiveness of the channel overall.

Key channel metrics include the following:

Average transaction size/value – This can be measured both in terms of the average transaction size for purchases by the intermediary and also the average purchase by the customer from the intermediary or store. Average transaction size measures the average financial value in whichever currency is used for each transaction. This metric is important as it helps the marketer to understand how successful the organisation has been in achieving higher sales from each customer. Ideally the average transaction size should increase, as this implies that the intermediary or the end customer is purchasing more from the organisation at each visit, which increases the organisation's efficiency and implies the customer is satisfied with the product or service. Marketers can deploy strategies to improve the average transaction size cost-effectively.

Average items per transaction – Understanding the number and type of items purchased in each transaction links to the average transaction size and, used in conjunction with it, gives marketers a good grasp of their customers' purchasing habits. For example, while the value of the average transaction may increase, if the average number of items per transaction increases at a higher rate, it means that customers are buying cheaper products. However, if the value of the average transaction increases at a higher rate than the average number of items per transaction, this means that customers are purchasing more, higher-value items. This metric also helps marketers to understand purchase patterns of the average customer, which links to their level of satisfaction with the organisation. For example, if a customer in a supermarket buys a lot of items in a single transaction it implies that they are happy with the store and that they do most of their shopping there, indicating a preference for that particular store. However, this does require further analysis.

Inventory turnover – It's important to measure inventory levels because having enough products 'on the shelf' is critical to customer satisfaction, but having too much stock can cause problems (particularly if goods are perishable). Inventory needs to be carefully managed in order to maintain optimum levels. Inventory turnover measures how quickly total inventory is sold and replaced. It is generally measured over the course of a year, but it can also be expressed in terms of the average number of days an item is held in stock before being sold. Turning over inventory as quickly as possible is important in keeping costs down, so marketers need strategies and tactics to help them manage the level. So, for example, if an organisation had sales of £200,000 and an average inventory value of £20,000, the stock turnover would be 10 (£200,000 divided by £20,000), meaning that the stock turns over ten times per year, or every 36.5 days on average.

Sales per unit of floor area – This is an important measure for retailers as it can show how efficiently they are using expensive retail space. The measure is usually applied only to the area specifically dedicated to selling, so stock rooms and other areas are not included. UK home entertainment retailer Richer Sounds has featured in the Guinness Book of Records for the past 20 years for having the highest sales per square foot of any retailer in the world in its London Bridge store. It is helped by the fact that it sells relatively high-value items, but it also uses its retail space highly efficiently, as anyone who has ever been into one of its stores will testify. As 'place' is an element of the marketing mix, and increasing sales is a marketing objective, the sales per unit of floor area is a key metric that can be used to measure the strategy's success.

Intermediary margin percentage – Intermediaries need to be successful in what they do and the margin they make is a measure of this success. Because intermediary costs can often be very high due to premises, staff, inventory and promotion costs, understanding the margins (a measure of profit, covered below) involved for intermediaries is critical. Without a satisfactory margin an intermediary would not want to continue to be involved with a product or service. The intermediary margin percentage is the difference between the price the intermediary paid for the product and the price they charge the end customer for it. Intermediaries need to make a profit to stay in business, but they also have to sell products from a particular supplier if their customers demand it. If a line is unprofitable for them they will either drop it from their range, if possible, or reduce promotional spending on it. Organisations supplying intermediaries therefore need strategies to help them maximise their margin.

D. MARGINS, PROFITS AND PROFITABILITY METRICS

In any commercial organisation the overriding objective is likely to be profit related. Profits enable a company to stay in business, because making a profit means that income exceeds expenditure. A company that consistently fails to make profits will run out of money and be unable to trade. There are different measures of profits and profitability and a marketer's ability to understand, discuss and apply these is essential to their credibility within the business.

While profit measures are critical in commercial businesses, they are equally important in not-for profit organisations. Overall objectives here don't typically include making a profit as such, but financial efficiency is very important and not-for-profit organisations are usually required to make a surplus income over expenditure. A charity, for example, is a typical not-for-profit organisation, and it relies on income in order to be able to provide the service it offers. If its income doesn't cover the expense involved in providing the service, then it's unlikely to survive. If it makes a surplus it can use this to provide additional services.

Key metrics for profits and profitability are:

Revenue – Also known as turnover, this is the income that the organisation receives from selling its products and services. Revenue is a leading indicator of performance as it indicates what has been sold in total. As such, it is a commonly used objective, and strategies are usually designed explicitly to increase revenue. But revenue is not an infallible measure of success as it may be achieved at too high a cost. Marketers should keep in mind the saying that 'turnover is vanity, profit is sanity', which implies that profit is the more reliable measure.

Gross profit – This is the measure of total revenue minus the costs incurred in producing the products that generate it. You can measure gross profit in two ways. For example, if someone buys an item for £100 and sells it for £150 the gross profit is £50 – the difference between the selling price and the purchase price. You could also express gross profit as a 'margin', which is the percentage of the selling price that is gross profit. In this case the margin is 33%, as £50 is 33% of the £150 selling price. High gross profits within a market sector indicate that an organisation is efficient. You can increase market share through low prices, but if the revenue you generate doesn't cover the costs involved in making and selling the products, you will sacrifice profitability. While improving gross profit should clearly be a key organisational objective, it represents only a partial picture of success, because it is calculated before the overhead expenditure needed to produce the product (research and development, marketing and sales costs etc).

Net profit – Whereas gross profit or margin takes into account only the cost of goods sold, the net profit figure is what is left when total costs are subtracted from total revenue. It is the final figure that you arrive at after subtracting from revenue all the taxes, selling costs, administrative costs, interest payments and so on that are associated with producing and selling the product. It is net profit that an organisation needs to survive, because the revenue has to cover all the costs of running the organisation.

Operating profit, or return on sales – This measures the organisation's ability to generate profit from sales. It is effectively the profit resulting from a sale, based on net profit but calculated before interest and tax as a percentage of total sales. An organisation needs sales to survive and profits to thrive. In order to understand the quality of the sales you need to measure the amount of profit generated from each unit of sales. Continuing the £50 gross profit example from above, if, in order to sell the item, the person had to place an advertisement at a cost of £10 and incurred other costs amounting to £10 before selling the product, the net profit is reduced to £30 and the net profit before tax margin is reduced to 20%. Return on sales is a more useful measure than net profit when used to compare different organisations or when considering profits over time, because with different sources of financial investment the interest payments can vary and this has implications for tax. Excluding interest and tax payments from the calculation allows for direct comparison and, from there, appropriate strategies to be determined.

	2016		2017	
	£	**%**	**£**	**%**
Sales/revenue	3000		2500	
Less cost of goods sold	(1200)		(900)	
Gross profit	1800	60%	1400	56%
Less operating expenses – sales, general admin, marketing etc.	(850)		(600)	
Operating profit	950	32%	800	32%
Interest	(200)		(150)	
Net profit before taxes (pretax income)	750	25%	650	26%
Tax	(360)		(200)	
Net profit	390	13%	400	16%

Fig 1.4 Measures of profitability

In this example you can see that the gross profit margin improved in 2016 to 60% from 56%, the operating profit remained the same at 32% and the net profit fell from 16% to 13%.

Return on investment (ROI) – This provides a snapshot of profitability, adjusted for the size of the investment assets tied up in the business. The calculation is:

Return on investment (%) = (net profit/investment) x 100.

For different analytical purposes you can employ different versions of ROI, including return on capital employed (ROCE) and return on net assets (RONA).

Many marketing activities, including, for example, new product development, website development and major promotional programmes, affect net profits, but may also require substantial capital investment in physical plant, IT systems or working capital to support increased inventory, therefore influencing return on investment. We consider ROI further in Chapter 3.

Sales funnel metrics – The sales funnel is a concept often related to digital marketing, and it considers the number of visitors to a website at the top level and those who convert to customers as the final stage at the bottom. A typical sales funnel could look like Fig 1.5, with numbers and percentages shown for each stage of the funnel process. The aim, of course, is to drive as many visitors as possible to the site and to persuade as many of those as possible to buy something.

Fig 1.5 The sales funnel

There are many metrics that you can apply within the funnel, but the key ones are:

- **Traffic sourcing and engagement** – Understanding where the traffic to the site comes from and how people are engaged. This is generally measured through web analytics packages. Understanding the source of business helps you to increase the flow into the top of the funnel.
- **Funnel value** – This represents the potential value of prospective customers in the funnel. If the 'normal' funnel conversion rates are understood, you can use this to estimate future income.
- **Call-to-action effectiveness** – Understanding how effective 'calls to action' on the site are, and why, will help you understand what makes visitors move to the next stage of the funnel and how to increase these numbers.
- **Time spent in each stage** – A very important measure because it builds understanding of future potential, and allows you to determine how to speed up the process.
- **Average sales value** – The average spend of website visitors, particularly if it is related to the costs involved in attracting and converting them, is a critical measure.

While sales funnel (or pipeline) metrics are used regularly in digital marketing, they are equally valid in offline marketing, where they are used to understand the number of actual and potential customers at various stages of the sales cycle. You should use metrics to determine the conversion rate of enquiries to sales at each stage of the pipeline, with typical stages being:

- Cold leads.
- Warm leads.
- Prospects.
- Quotations.
- Sales.

By measuring the numbers of customers generated from each stage of the pipeline you can calculate the potential future sales based on the number of potential customers at each stage at any given time. For example:

- Cold leads – 500
- Warm leads – 150
- Prospects – 25
- Quotations – 10
- Orders won – 5

In this example, we would need a pipeline starting with 100 cold leads to generate every order received. This information, combined with the average time it takes to move a customer from one stage to the next and the numbers currently at each stage, can help you to determine your sales strategies.

ACTIVITY 5
Calculate the sales funnel metrics for the online activity of your own organisation or, if you don't have an online operation, do it for one that you are familiar with – Amazon would be a good example. Consider ways the performance may be improved and what the targets should be.

E. PRODUCT AND PORTFOLIO METRICS

While marketers tend to include service and other intangibles within the overall definition of 'product', customers don't see things the same way. They just buy something that satisfies a need or desire – so 'a solution' – but they also want 'value' from it, and value is a combination of quality and cost. Marketers need to understand how well their products and services perform against these two critical customer criteria, and, by extension, how successful new products are and the impact that one product in the range has on another.

Key metrics for product and portfolio understanding are:

Usage – This is about understanding how products at different price levels are used. A product offering superior performance can command a premium price, for example. There is no specific formula for usage, but it involves assessing the maximum financial benefits an organisation can gain from providing a product or service, while at the same time giving substantial value to the customer. 'Value' takes into account the purchase price along with the cost of usage, maintenance and implementation of the product or service, as well as the benefit it confers.

REAL LIFE
Volkswagen announced that it would be selling the world's most fuel-efficient car, the XL1, which would do 313 miles to the gallon (less than 1 litre per 100km) with emissions of just 21g/km of CO_2. This meant that customers would have very low operating costs. However, the car was very expensive to buy – nearly £100,000 in the UK – which meant that the total perceived value could be low as the purchase price more than offset the savings in running costs. Unsurprisingly, Volkswagen expected to sell only 200 XL1s.

Marketing cost per unit – As budgets are always limited the money allocated needs to be used as effectively as possible. A simple calculation of marketing expense divided by sales volume gives the marketing cost associated with each unit. Marketing cost per unit declines over time: the product lifecycle shows that the highest costs are usually at the introduction phase, when costs are high but product take-up is low. However, sales increase over time and the product needs less and less marketing expenditure support. In very competitive times the marketing cost per unit may increase due to the need to defend market share from competitors.

New product adoption rate/percentage of total sales represented by new products – New products are important to help keep organisations relevant to changing customer demand, and the extent to which those new products are adopted demonstrates the success of new product development activity. The adoption rate helps marketers to determine strategies to maximise the product life and sales during the product lifecycle.

Cannibalisation rates – New or improved products can have an impact on the sales of existing products, and the cannibalisation rate is the rate at which new product sales are stealing sales from the existing product line. It is generally expressed as a percentage. Understanding the cannibalisation rate can help marketers plan activities to support both new and existing products, and to time the introduction of new products carefully in order to minimise the cannibalisation rate and maximise the profitability of both new and existing products.

F. PRICING METRICS, INCLUDING STRATEGY AND TACTICS

Once a product category has been selected, price has more influence than any other element in the marketing mix. The price charged has to be reflected in the product quality, the promotional messages and media used, the channels employed and the support offered through the extended marketing mix elements. Price is also the element of the marketing mix that most directly relates to profit, so the pricing strategy employed has to ensure that all costs are recovered.

The key pricing metrics are as follows:

Sales price variation – This measures the difference over time between the actual price charged and the recommended price for each unit. The actual price charged for a product often varies from the recommended price due to actions from competitors, other market conditions or more strategic reasons. Price variations are particularly common in business-to business-marketing, where prices are often set individually for customers and price lists are not available. In retail environments, products that are marked down in end-of-season sales show a variance from the recommended price. Similarly, a 'bundled' deal, which combines multiple products into a package with a price lower than the total of the individual prices, would also be classed as a sales price variation. In strategy terms, the sales price variance may indicate the recommended price is incorrect – if all products have to be discounted then maybe a lower price should have been set initially. However, price discounting can obviously be a specific promotional tool, in which case the variance would be planned for.

Profit impact – This measures the cash contribution per unit at different projected levels of sale, taking into account fixed and variable manufacturing costs, the necessary promotional marketing spend and pricing. Profit impact is a metric used as part of pricing strategy, ensuring the optimum price is set.

Price premium – Also known as the **brand premium**, this is the additional amount customers pay for a branded product over a weaker brand or a commodity product.

Price elasticity of demand – This measures how responsive demand is to a change in price. If demand for a product changes very little with price changes, that product is described as 'price inelastic', but if demand changes considerably the product is 'price elastic'. For example, if demand falls by 10% with a 2% increase in price, elasticity is -5 – demonstrating elastic demand. A product's price elasticity may be determined by the uniqueness of a product or the availability of substitutes. Where demand is elastic, an organisation can consider lowering the price to sell more, providing that the desired profit is also achieved – and a profit impact calculation can support such a decision.

G. PROMOTIONAL AND MEDIA METRICS

When most people think of marketing, they think primarily in terms of advertising and promotion, and these are traditionally the hardest areas to measure because of the lack of direct linkages between mass media promotion and the results they deliver. But however difficult it might be to quantify the link, it's important to try, and marketers can choose from a plethora of methods and metrics which, used properly, can deliver accurate results. However, because all the different promotional elements of a campaign work together in synergy to deliver the overall result, you have to ensure you measure the integrated communications – including the media you use.

Key metrics for promotion include:

Share of voice – This measures an organisation's media spend on a product compared with the total expenditure for the product category in the marketplace. In a crowded place someone who talks very little or very softly is unlikely to be noticed, and it can be the same with marketing communication. In order for a message to be heard in a crowded marketplace it needs to have a significant share of voice. For example, you would calculate Samsung's share of voice for its Galaxy S range of smartphones by working out first what it spends on promoting the range and then what percentage that represents of the total promotional spend on all smartphones by every manufacturer in the sector (Apple, HTC, Sony etc). But while higher share of voice may build greater awareness, it is not a complete measure. Factors such as the message and how memorable it is, or the media used to promote it, may have a larger effect than the direct spend would indicate.

Recall – This is a test of overall brand awareness or advertising impact. It's unlikely that a one-off promotional message would get much attention, so most promotion requires a series of 'opportunities to see' an advertisement, or equivalent, as part of a campaign. Establishing whether customers recall a recent campaign is an important metric to assess the validity/effectiveness of campaigns. Recall is measured in two ways:

- **Top of mind** – The first brand recalled in a sector.
- **Dominance** – The only brand recalled.

Measured through research, recall can be determined through 'aided recall' – that is, a customer is shown an advertisement and asked if they remember it – or 'unaided recall' – where customers are asked about what they remember having seen without any stimulus. Marketers aim for high recall levels and make decisions to improve the targeting and message of promotion to increase recall.

Recognition – Related to recall, recognition measures whether a customer remembers the organisation, advert or product when they are shown the advert again. Assessed through research, recognition asks whether the customer has been exposed to the brand.

Response rate – This is the number of people responding to an advert, promotional message or offer. While a customer may have seen an advert, remember it and recognise the product, most promotion is ultimately aimed at getting the customer to respond in some way. High response rates are obviously desirable. The response rate is generally easy to measure in direct marketing and online activity, but for offline response you could use a number of different methods, so it is best to see what works in order to build more successful future campaigns.

Conversion rate – This means conversion from enquiries to orders. The conversion rate is the percentage of prospective customers who purchase products from the organisation. Organisations aim for a high conversion rate, and understanding the steps involved and how to increase the conversion at each step in the sales funnel is a key requirement for successful marketing.

Redemption rates – In any promotion that involves a direct offer, such as a coupon, the redemption rate is important to measure as it is a direct result of the activity. The redemption rate measures the percentage of coupons redeemed out of the total number issued. An example would be a coffee shop providing a coupon entitling a customer to a free drink for every ten purchased. The number of customers who use the coupon to gain the free drink out of all the coupons issued demonstrates the success of the campaign and the effectiveness of the coupon as a promotional tool.

Reach – This is the number or percentage of people reached by (or 'exposed to') an advertisement or promotional campaign over a specified period of time. As a promotion is used to appeal to a particular audience marketers want to know the proportion of the target audience reached. 'Exposure' is defined as an opportunity to see or hear a particular advertisement.

H. DIGITAL METRICS

The advent of digital marketing has been accompanied by greater measurement of marketing activity. This is partly because it is relatively easy to measure online marketing, and partly to do with the broader issue of growing marketing accountability. The number of metrics available for measuring online marketing has raised awareness generally of the need to measure marketing, and digital measures have become drivers for wider marketing metrics, which has helped to align online and offline measures, as we explain in Chapter 5.

Key digital metrics are as follows:

Page impressions – This measures the number of visitors to the website, often broken down into new visitors and repeat visitors. Numbers of visitors to a website is an indication of the interest consumers have in the organisation and its products, because whereas a customer may see an offline ad whether they want to or not, a visit to a website is a deliberate action.

Total clicks – Many organisations see communication and engagement with customers on social media as beneficial in itself, but the real measure of success is the number of people who then go on to visit the website. Total clicks measures this in relation to the word-of-mouth generated from social media activity. High total clicks indicate that the customer is not just talking about the organisation, but engaging positively with it.

Cost per order – Whether companies use 'pay per click' or banner advertising they incur a cost in promoting themselves. Cost per order measures the value of orders generated online against the promotional cost required to generate them.

Cost per click – Not all enquiries become orders, and the cost per click measures the visits to the website against the advertising costs incurred to encourage them there.

Social media activity – Social media sites such as Facebook, Twitter and LinkedIn may generate a number of followers (or the equivalent) for the organisation but not all of these followers engage with it in any meaningful way. However, customer activity in itself is a measure of their interest. Understanding social media activity helps an organisation to understand whether its products and services are relevant to customers. Companies can measure the number of active 'members' – that is, those who engage with the company through social media – as a proportion of total members (followers). Measuring social media sentiment can also yield valuable insight about how customers view your brand, your business, your marketing, even your social media strategy itself. There are a number of different sentiment analysis tools to help you do this, including Hootsuite Insights, Twitter Advanced Search, Brandwatch, Semantria and Rapidminer. https://blog.hootsuite.com/social-media-sentiment-analysis-tools/

See more on social media sentiment in section 5.5.

Bounce rates – A key measure for websites, the bounce rate is the number of visitors to a website who leave after visiting just one page. A high bounce rate may indicate that the web page doesn't meet customers' requirements – there's nothing on the site that makes them want to explore further. Bounce rate tends to be a standard feature of web analytics. Improving the bounce rate is a priority for digital marketers, who want to encourage visitors to explore more and move to the later stages of the sales funnel (see Chapter 3).

Downloads – If a visitor downloads something from a website it indicates an interest in the organisation's offer, so is an important metric of engagement. Downloads can be measured as the percentage of visitors to the site who download additional information, hopefully providing contact information when they do so.

1.3

Developing appropriate KPIs

As we have seen in section 1.2, marketers have many metrics to choose from. To avoid drowning in data it's important to select a few 'key performance indicators' (KPIs) that are critical for your particular business and that will allow you to monitor whether or not you are on track. Focusing on a few critical areas will also ensure that things get done. While every business's KPIs will be different, Marr (2014) offers some useful KPI dos and don'ts.

Do	Don't
Start with your strategy	Measure simply because other companies do
Define the questions you need an answer to	Only measure what is easy to collect
Customise KPIs to your needs	Let your KPIs get out of date
Ensure the KPIs are owned and understood by people in your organisation	Hard-wire your KPIs to incentive systems
Use KPIs to improve performance	Use KPIs as a command and control tool

Fig 1.6 *Adapted from Marr, 2014*

Effective team structures

One of the big benefits of KPIs is that they can focus everyone in the business, not just the marketing function, on what needs to be done. Here Marr's point about ensuring KPIs are owned and understood by everyone in the organisation is key. Because, of course, marketing metrics are rarely generated and used solely by the marketing function. The most effective structure for allowing everyone to generate, implement and use marketing metrics is the matrix.

A matrix organisation crosses vertical functional divisions with horizontal product, customer or project teams (see Fig 1.7). Matrix organisations typically have fewer horizontal divisions than in traditional hierarchical organisations. In some cases horizontal divisions are removed completely to facilitate fully-integrated cross-functional teams. Cross-functional teams are made up of representatives from all the key areas in any particular customer, project or product group, and team members are given responsibilities that require them to work with members of other functions while retaining some allegiance to their primary function. The team members report to a line manager within their function but also to the leader of the cross-functional team.

If a team were set up to implement marketing metrics, for example, the marketer on the team would report to the marketing manager and to the leader of the metrics implementation team. Likewise, the person responsible for the IT elements of metrics implementation would report to the IT manager and to the leader of the metrics implementation team.

It is these horizontal and vertical relationships that form the matrix.

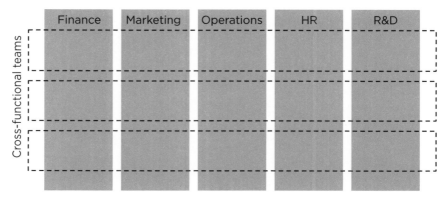

Fig 1.7 A matrix organisation structure.

A matrix is not just an organisational structure; it is also a way of approaching the challenges facing the business. It allows complex tasks such as implementing, using and managing marketing metrics to be tackled in a highly collaborative, integrated fashion, encouraging the cross-fertilisation of ideas and a high degree of co-ordination. The structure breaks down the traditional 'silo' approach to working, where allegiances are up and down the hierarchy rather than across departments or to the organisation as a whole. Silo working encourages functional 'fiefdoms' and does not foster the kind of customer-oriented cultures that best guarantee business success.

Matrix structures support workflow management and lead to better decision-making. Bringing together different perspectives from different functions helps to solve problems by reducing the power of individual departmental specialisations and allowing the team to see the bigger picture. As a result metrics contain multiple inputs. Horizontal workflows typically mean that bureaucratic obstacles are removed too.

REAL LIFE
Until 2012 the advertising team at Facebook was responsible for the advertising products, and the product teams were responsible for creating and refining the user experience. Founder Mark Zuckerberg kept the teams separate because he believed that the product team

should focus only on the consumer's experience, without being distracted by financial concerns. The ad team was rewarded for increasing revenue, while the product teams were assessed based on user-engagement metrics.

But a number of key players within the company began to argue that if all the teams were rewarded for contributing to revenue, the enterprise would generate not just more ideas, but also better, more creative and more diverse ideas. The management structure was changed so that now, for example, the News Feed product team is accountable for how much money comes through News Feed advertising, and the mobile product team is expected to generate ideas to make money through mobile advertising.

The impact of the decision to change the management structure was profound, precipitating as it did a fundamental rethink in the business about how to make adverts feel like a well-integrated experience. Integrating the teams led to it running ads within its apps' News Feed, which, in turn, led to its first breakthrough mobile-advertising product. Some ascribe Facebook's rebound after its market capitalisation halved in the wake of its IPO in May 2012, to this single decision.

Source: Carr, A. (2014)

Workflow management

The term 'workflow' describes the tasks, steps and actions taken by people within organisations that require inputs and produce outputs through the use of resources available. Workflow management therefore involves developing and delivering repeatable patterns of activity through organising and utilising the resources for the processes that transform the inputs to the desired outputs. In the context of marketing metrics, workflow management is a process for delivering the data and information to inform the metrics reporting system. These sequences of operations deliver outputs through a repeatable process, providing consistent, reliable outcomes.

The most important function of a workflow management system is the way it co-ordinates the different components of the workflow. This is invaluable when it comes to marketing metrics, given that many sources of information need to be co-ordinated to produce individual metrics, and that the metrics need to work together to provide a complete picture.

Most workflow management is conducted using software. When developing metrics systems these need to be integrated into the software systems to enable the rapid delivery of the required content and reports. However, within small organisations or teams workflow management can be done manually.

Aligning marketing and sales

The respective roles and relative dominance of the sales and marketing functions have been a source of debate for many years. To an extent it depends on the nature of the organisation, but whatever the relationship between the two disciplines it is important that they are aligned in order to provide metrics that will allow the organisation to sell more of its products and services.

The Chartered Institute of Marketing White Paper *Marketing and Sales Fusion* (2011) looks at the benefits to organisations of integrating the two functions. It's worth considering a quote in the White Paper by US marketing authority Philip Kotler:

"When sales are disappointing, marketing blames the sales force for its poor execution of an otherwise brilliant rollout plan. The sales team, in turn, claims that marketing sets prices too high and uses too much of the budget, which instead should go towards hiring more sales people or paying the sales reps higher commissions. More broadly, sales departments tend to believe that marketers are out of touch with what's really going on with customers. Marketing believes the sales force is myopic – too focused on individual customer experiences, insufficiently aware of the larger market, and blind to its future. In short, each group often undervalues the other's contributions."

Many of the issues Kotler highlights can be overcome by integrating sales and marketing metrics. Integrating sales metrics relating to turnover and areas such as the numbers of deals and opportunities created, with marketing metrics demonstrating the incremental contribution and return on investment of marketing programmes, can be very powerful, because each side helps the other to their mutual benefit and the benefit of the organisation as a whole.

The White Paper also reports that Rolls-Royce has never had separate sales and marketing functions, stating that the result of bespoke project teams made up of both sales and marketing is good for business. Where sales and marketing are integrated, according to the White Paper, everything benefits – information flows are enhanced, return on investment (ROI) is more accurate, strategic direction-setting is improved, and so on. Professor Alan Tapp, professor of social marketing at Bristol Business School, states in the White Paper that "a fragmented marketing and sales team makes customer relationship management harder, is an obstacle to retaining customers in a cross-channel world where the customer needs to be pulled rather than pushed, [makes it] harder to accurately measure ROI, and [makes] value-chain thinking harder to calculate."

Also in the White Paper, Holger Ernst, professor of technology and innovation management at the WHU – Otto Beisheim Graduate School of Management, comments on the effect of integrated sales and marketing on new product development (NPD): "Because of their different departmental orientations, marketing and sales provide complementary information that is valuable for the NPD process. Marketing provides strategic marketing information, while sales provides specific customer information. Combining this information is critical because it helps avoid niche solutions for an individual customer that, in turn, neglect the attractiveness of larger market segments or market trends or are not aligned with the firm's overall product portfolio."

See more on this subject in section 2.1.

Reporting techniques and key marketing metrics

There are many ways to report metrics, the most common being dashboards, which we cover in detail in Chapter 4. But the format in which metrics are reported is less important than the content of the metrics and the frequency with which they are reported. Good decisions are built on robust information, and before marketers even start to decide what metrics to develop they need to understand exactly what information executives need – but they must assume that whatever the information, executives need it in a great amount of detail.

CRM

Technology – and CRM systems in particular – can help marketing measure its performance against KPIs, resulting in improved efficiency and effectiveness, higher productivity, improved accountability and responsiveness, better market intelligence, enhanced customer experience and engagement, and so on.

Marketing performance management (MPM) software allows companies to measure, analyse and optimise their marketing resources, analyse and report on their marketing performance, and improve outcomes over time through 'closed-loop' marketing. It also helps marketers to identify what KPIs to focus on and whether and when to change those KPIs.

1.4

THE RISKS OF POORLY IMPLEMENTED METRICS

Marketers often spend a great deal of time and effort trying to work out the right factors to measure, whether in terms of marketing efficiency, effectiveness or performance. But they often end up making the wrong selection – and measuring the wrong things can be more dangerous than measuring nothing at all.

Using the wrong metric – One of the main problems is that they can't find the right metric to measure what they need to measure, so they end up using a poor substitute. The substitute metric may be less relevant to the original measurement requirement and therefore provide inaccurate and unreliable results. For example, it may be relatively straightforward to measure sales generated from a direct marketing campaign, but measuring the right factors in social media can be much more problematic, as the Real Life example below demonstrates.

REAL LIFE

Organisations might be set up to measure the profitability of customers on some of their social media platforms, but they need to exercise caution when adding new elements into the mix. For example, measuring the value of public interaction with the organisation's tweets is very different from counting the number of 'likes' on its Facebook site. Trying to make direct comparisons between these two metrics could result in the marketer providing misleading data to senior management as to which social media platforms are more profitable, therefore distorting the organisation's digital marketing portfolio planning process.

Measuring the wrong thing – When marketers can't decide what they really need to measure, they measure something else instead. For example they might use basic customer satisfaction data to determine a Net Promoter Score® (which we discussed in section 1.2B), but basic customer satisfaction data is unlikely to provide the customer advocacy metrics that are required to classify customers as 'promoters', 'passives' or 'detractors' as determined by the NPS® model.

Using the wrong data – Marketers may be given inappropriate sources of data from which to draw measurable conclusions. For example, as Kotler and Keller (2006) state: "Senior managers want to know the outcomes and revenues relating from communications investments. Too often, however, their communications directors supply only outputs and expenses: press clipping counts, number of ads placed, media costs."

To ensure they are measuring the right things, using the right data and creating the right metrics, marketers first need to define what objectives they are trying to meet. Typical objectives might include, for example, driving increased sales, attracting prospective customers via marketing campaigns, or persuading online customers to spend more time on the website. The specific measurement objectives should drive the choice of factors to be measured – hence the need to focus on KPIs, as we discussed above

Incorrect measurement and metrics can result in both marketing and business failure. For example, a selected metric might not simply fail to tell the organisation what it needs to know, but actually lead it down the wrong path, with potentially disastrous consequences.

REAL LIFE

The marketing manager of a wine bar wants to track the number of visits to the website in order to find ways of driving new business. She may discover high numbers of page hits, but a significant proportion of those visitors could be under the legal drinking age, so are highly unlikely to visit the wine bar and be converted into real customers. So while a site visit metric on its own might yield positive results, relying on this exclusively would result in the business failing to achieve its sales forecasts. To obtain reliable information on which to base future business decisions, this metric would need to be overlaid by another one that profiles the demographics of site visitors.

Measuring too often or too infrequently – This can also have damaging consequences. For example, most organisations measure sales and customer satisfaction regularly, ranging from weekly to annually. Let's imagine that an organisation's website has crashed for a few hours during one particular week. If that organisation usually measures customer satisfaction and sales metrics over the short term it might assume it needs to make significant changes to the products or services it sells on the site, or to the way it responds to customer enquiries. But either of these strategies could represent a serious error of marketing judgement.

If the organisation takes a longer-term view, however, and looks at the average measurement of sales and/or customer satisfaction over a month, quarter or year, it would see that the website crash was a temporary aberration, and that no realignments are needed.

Metrics need to be used at a frequency that allows for immediate adjustments where necessary, while at the same time providing the all-important bigger picture.

Confusing quantity and quality – A common error in business-to-business marketing is to rate quantity over quality. For example, neither the volume of online sales campaign leads nor the number of business cards collected at a trade show are, on their own, a reliable measure of potential future business because they take no account of the quality of those leads. Many of them may be of no real value to the organisation as potential customers, so using them as a basis for segmentation and targeting will be a waste of marketing time and money.

Relying on single sources of metrics – This usually produces misleading information. Factors that are easy to understand get over-used, even if they are not relevant. Such factors are often referred to as **'vanity metrics'** because they appear to be robust and valuable, but are meaningful only in certain contexts. For example, many organisations starting to use social media place great faith in single metrics such as the number of followers they have on LinkedIn or Twitter, or the number of 'likes' they get on Facebook. But unless those followers actively engage with the organisation and advocate what it does via word-of-mouth or viral marketing, the organisation will enjoy no measurable increase in sales, customer retention or new business. Marketers need to use a set of different metrics in order to draw useful insights from the results they present.

Taking into account margins of error – When applying marketing metrics, marketers also have to consider the margin of error. The world of political marketing provides examples. When pollsters estimate election results they build in a margin of error based on assumptions about who might end up not voting, who might switch their intentions at the last minute, and so on. This margin of error is a guide to how statistically significant early polls actually are. For example, 60% of respondents polled might state their intention to vote for a particular party. But if the margin of error is 5%, this is not very meaningful, because it implies that anywhere between 55-65% of respondents would realistically vote for that party. Such a wide margin of error would make it very difficult for the political marketer to draw firm conclusions from the poll about the true percentage of voters likely to vote for his or her party.

You tend to get wider margins of error the smaller the sample group you research and the more random the sample – both of which tend to apply with political polls. Any assumptions based on a random sample are likely to be flawed. You can reduce the margin of error by increasing the sample size, or by researching separate control groups. Control groups consist of groups of respondents where the marketer separates the target population into two groups, which are similar, but which differ in a specific aspect (for example, male and female). Any significant difference between the two groups in terms of the response to a given question indicates the importance of the specific variable (male or female in this case) to each group.

In political marketing, for example, where a margin of error of more than 3% would be regarded as inconclusive, you would typically require around 1,000 respondents to reduce the margin of error to a more acceptable 2-3%. The larger the control group, the lower the margin of error experienced, and the higher the confidence levels the political marketer can have in the poll results.

Service-level agreements – Marketers also need to exercise caution with service-level agreements (SLAs), whether they are drawing them up for suppliers, or are suppliers themselves. Poorly thought-through SLAs can contain inappropriate, misleading (and, therefore, ultimately controversial) metrics. The factors measured in an SLA have to be as relevant as possible to the key service objectives in order to avoid disappointing results and associated costs.

Typical metrics used in SLA measurement may include:

- Service availability – Such as telecommunications network uptime.
- Percentage of defects – In manufactured products and parts, for example.
- Level of security breaches – On, for example, websites or mobile applications, particularly for financial services organisations such as retail banks.

To be meaningful, such factors need to be precisely quantifiable through detailed and specific metrics. This allows customers to monitor whether SLA terms are being met, and, if not, whether they may claim compensation or other penalties under the terms specified in the agreement. In practice, many companies make SLA factors so difficult to measure that it deters customers from applying for compensation, increasingly the likelihood that those customers will vote with their feet and take their business elsewhere.

ACTIVITY 6

Ask key colleagues in the customer service, operations or sales functions of your organisation what metrics, if any, they use to measure key customer criteria, and what the underlying objectives of those metrics are. Evaluate with your colleagues whether you think these metrics need to change in the light of changing market or customer trends.

If metrics are not currently used, which ones should be used and what would be the objectives for them? What dangers might there be in introducing new metrics, particularly if they are poorly implemented?

1.5

Internal barriers to change

As we pointed out in section 1.3, marketing metrics are typically generated and used not only by the marketing department, but by everyone in the organisation. Indeed, in a customer-centric organisation it is critical that everyone is aligned around metrics that are designed to delight customers profitably.

However, this is easier said than done. Many organisations still operate in silos, and traditional tension between, for example, sales and marketing, and marketing and finance, dies hard in some places. But well-chosen KPIs, which connect everyone to the company's mission, vision, desired customer experience and financial performance, can actually help to break down departmental boundaries and help employees understand how they do and can contribute.

To arrive at this organisational nirvana marketers need to surmount a number of barriers. CEOs and finance directors want marketers to demonstrate their effectiveness through the use of metrics, but the organisational culture has to support this.

- Marketers need to be able to demonstrate to senior executives where a focus on short-term financial results may threaten longer-term customer loyalty – and, therefore, sustainable financial performance.
- Marketers should do as much brand marketing inside the company – including communicating about the value of metrics – as they do outside it. They have to win over other functions, not tell them what to do.
- Processes need to be redesigned in order to satisfy customers, rather than for the convenience of people inside the organisation.

It is, to some extent, a case of chicken and egg here. For marketers to prove the effectiveness of marketing, they need everyone to sign up to common customer-oriented metrics – but they need to persuade them to do that in the first place. The answer is to focus initially on a few simple profitability-focused metrics where they can demonstrate quick wins.

The Mendelow Stakeholder Matrix

If marketers are to win over others in the organisation to a customer-centric approach underpinned by common KPIs they have to understand the different stakeholders within the organisation and their differing priorities, claims and levels of influence. A useful tool for gaining this understanding is the Mendelow Stakeholder Matrix, which helps categorise people according to their power over and interest in the organisation's affairs. You can then determine what strategy to adopt towards them. For example, you might need to invest minimal effort in those with low power and low interest, and focus most of your attention on the key players who are most interested and wield most power. Beware though – stakeholders can move around the map, so you need to monitor your communication accordingly.

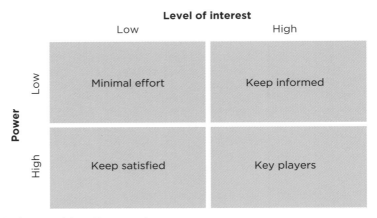

Fig 1.8 The Mendelow Framework

The McKinsey 7-S Framework

The McKinsey 7-S Framework is another valuable tool that can be used to configure the organisation around a customer focus, supported by metrics. The model, named after the consulting firm McKinsey & Co which developed it, encompasses all the elements of organisation design and how they fit together.

- **Strategy** – Encompasses the overall position of the organisation and its long-term direction.
- **Structure** – Defines the formal roles of employees within the strategy, including their responsibilities and reporting lines. The main structural forms include matrix, multidivisional and functional.
- **Systems** – The various formal and informal processes that rule and support people inside and outside an organisation. These include budgeting systems, marketing information systems, training systems, cost accounting procedures etc, which support the day-to-day running of the organisation
- **Staff** – The different types of people within the organisation, and the systems of reward, recruitment and socialisation used to develop them. Organisations need the right people for the strategy they are following, and, particularly where the organisational structure is being altered, it is vital that department heads have the appropriate abilities.
- **Style** – An organisation's leadership style can take various forms, including autocratic, participative, collaborative and coercive. It is signalled by how the top managers spend their time, and their

symbolic behaviour. Leadership style needs to fit will with the culture of the organisation – so, for example, a participative or collaborative style is much more likely to achieve results in matrix structure organisation.

- **Skills** – Employees' talents should be developed into the capabilities required by the organisational strategy through training, improved information technology and rewards.
- **Superordinate goals (or shared values)** – Are the goals that form the overall purpose of the organisation and drive it forward. They encompass its vision, values and objectives.

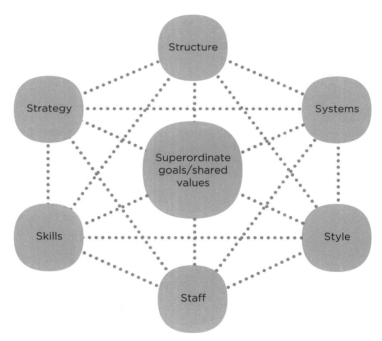

Fig 1.9 McKinsey's – S Framework

McKinsey's 7-S framework draws attention to at least three organisational features.

1. It shows that every one of the 7-S elements has many aspects and highlights how all these aspects need to fit together. There is more to organising than simply getting the correct structure.
2. The framework also shows that if one of the main elements is changed then the other elements will have to be changed as well in order to preserve the correct alignment.

Changing single elements is likely to cause disruption until the point that the other elements are aligned accordingly.

QUICK QUIZ – CHECK YOUR KNOWLEDGE

Questions

1. Why is measuring marketing activity becoming more important in today's business environment?
2. What are the three elements of 'the triple bottom line'?
3. What is the difference between metrics and analytics?
4. Why would the number of followers an organisation has on LinkedIn or Twitter, or the number of 'likes' it gets on Facebook, be classified as 'vanity' measures?
5. Which three stakeholder groups do CIMA say integrated reporting can benefit?
6. Name three typical metrics used for service-level agreements.
7. What does McDonald identify as the five criteria of a segment?
8. Name the three categories customers are grouped into with the Net Promoter Score® measurement.
9. What is the churn rate?
10. If an organisation buys a product for £80 and sells it for £120 what is the gross profit margin?
11. Why is sales per unit of floor area an important measure for retailers?
12. If demand changes very little with price changes, is it elastic or inelastic demand?

Answers

1. Inter-functional trust, understanding and conflict resolution; marketing becoming hard-edged; fewer resources available; more easily accessible data.
2. People, planet and profit or social, environmental and economic.
3. Analytics are the tools that are used to provide data for the metrics.
4. Counting passive followers would not on its own result in a measurable increase in sales, customer retention or new business.
5. Investors, employees and other stakeholders.
6. Service availability, percentage of defects, level of security breaches.
7. It must be identifiable and recognisable, exist independently, be measurable, be substantial and be externally accessible and actionable.
8. Promoters, passives, detractors.
9. The rate at which a company loses customers.
10. 33% – the profit is £40 (selling price of £120 less cost of £80), which is 33% of the £120 selling price.
11. It demonstrates how effectively retail space is being used.
12. Inelastic.

BIBLIOGRAPHY

ACCA (2015) All about stakeholders – Part 1. http://www.accaglobal.com/uk/en/student/exam-support-resources/professional-exams-study-resources/p1/technical-articles/stakeholders-part1.html

Anon (ND) Definition of greenwashing. *FT.com*. http://lexicon.ft.com/Term?term=green-washing

Anon (2009)The triple bottom line. It consists of three Ps: profit, people and planet. *The Economist*. http://www.economist.com/node/14301663

Ansoff, I. (1957) Strategies for diversification. *Harvard Business Review*, Vol35(2). pp13-124.

Berrone, P. (2016) How to succeed at sustainability (and why greenwashing doesn't work) *Forbes*, 15 September.

Brand Finance (2017) Global 500 2017: The world's most valuable brands of 2017. http://brandirectory.com/league_tables/table/global-500-2017

Carr, A. (2014) Facebook everywhere. *Fast Company*, 16 June. https://www.fastcompany.com/3031237/facebook-everywhere

CIM (2007) *The good, the bad and the indifferent – marketing and the triple bottom line*. White Paper. https://www.cim.co.uk/media/4888/triple-bottom-line-booklet_web.pdf

CIM (2011) *Sales and marketing fusion*. White Paper. https://www.cim.co.uk/media/4887/1259ri_wp_mktgsalesfusion_web.pdf

CIMA (2014) Tomorrow's business success: using integrated reporting to help create value and effectively tell the full story. Chartered Institute of Management Accountants. http://www.cimaglobal.com/Documents/Thought_leadership_docs/reporting/Tomorrows-Business-Success-Integrated-Reporting-guide.pdf

Farris, P.W., Bendle, N.T., Pfeifer, P.E. and Reibstein, D.J. (2010) *Key marketing metrics: the 50+ metrics every manager needs to know*. Harlow, Pearson.

Fortein, D. (2017) Sentiment analysis tools for social media marketers. *Hootsuite*. https://blog.hootsuite.com/social-media-sentiment-analysis-tools/

IIRC (2013) The International <IR> Framework. The International Integrated Reporting Council. 37 pages. http://www.theiirc.org/wp-content/uploads/2013/12/13-12-08-THE-INTERNATIONAL-IR-FRAMEWORK-2-1.pdf

Interbrand (2017) Best global brands 2016 rankings. http://interbrand.com/best-brands/best-global-brands/2016/ranking/

Kotler, P., Armstrong, G., Saunders, J. and Wong, V. (1999) *Principles of marketing*. 2nd edition, New Jersey, Prentice Hall.

Kotler, P. and Keller, K. (2006) *Marketing management*. 12th edition, New Jersey, Prentice Hall.

Kotter, J (2013) When CEOs talk strategy, 70% of the company doesn't get it. *Forbes.* http://www.forbes.com/sites/johnkotter/2013/07/09/heres-why-ceo-strategies-fall-on-deaf-ears/

Lautman, M.R and Pauwels, K. (2009) Metrics that matter. *Journal of Advertising Research,* Sept, Vol49(3), pp339-359.

Manyika, J. et al (2011) Big data: the next frontier for innovation, competition, and productivity. McKinsey Global Institute, May. http://www.mckinsey.com/insights/business_technology/big_data_the_next_frontier_for_innovation

McDonald, M. and Wilson, H. (2011) *Marketing plans: how to prepare them, how to use them.* 7th edition. Chichester, John Wiley.

McDonald, M. (2004) Market segmentation: how to do it, how to profit from it. Oxford, Butterworth-Heinemann.

McDonald, M and Mouncey, P. (2009) *Marketing accountability: a new metrics model to measure marketing effectiveness.* London, Kogan Page.

McMeeken, R. (2012) The National Trust: a fresh start. *The Marketer,* March, pp22-24.

Marr, B. (2014) 25 need to know key performance indicators. Harlow, Pearson.

Norman W. and MacDonald, C. (2003) Getting to the bottom of 'triple bottom line'. *Business Ethics Quarterly* 31 pages. https://www.cambridge.org/core/journals/business-ethics-quarterly/article/getting-to-the-bottom-of-triple-bottom-line/A7D95AB81098B4701947C999AE720697

Palmer, R., Cockton, J. and Cooper, G. (2007) *Managing marketing: marketing success through good management practice.* Oxford, Elsevier.

Reichheld, F.F. (2003) The one number you need to grow. *Harvard Business Review,* Dec, Vol81(12), pp46-54.

Sorger, S. (2013) *Marketing analytics*. 1st edition, Admiral Press.

Wilson, R. and Gilligan, C. (2009) *Strategic marketing management.* 3rd edition, Oxford, Elsevier.

WPP (2017) BrandZ Most valuable global brands 2017. http://www.wpp.com/wpp/marketing/brandz/brandz-2017/

2.0
ASSESSMENT OF DATA FOR MARKETING ANALYSIS

OUTLINE

This chapter explains why it is so important for marketers to understand the breadth and depth of data that is available and assess its worth. At the end of this chapter you will be able to:

- Understand in more detail the sources of data for marketing and sales analysis.
- Understand how data can work together to produce a bigger picture.
- Assess the strengths and weaknesses of data sources.

2.1

RESOURCES OF DATA FOR MARKETING ANALYSIS IDENTIFYING BEST USE, STRENGTHS AND WEAKNESSES

Metrics help marketers in a variety of ways. They help them to understand consumer behaviour and the effect of their marketing activities, enable them to make more informed decisions and allow them to demonstrate the impact of marketing on overall business results – justifying further investment in marketing and winning credibility within the business in the process. The understanding gained from using advanced analytics helps to increase return on marketing investment and fosters organisational growth.

We list some of the main sources of data for marketing decision-making below.

Brand research

Organisations produce products or services, but customers buy and engage with brands – and as products and services proliferate, the stronger your brand is the more likely it is to stand out and be competitive. Marketing's primary role is to generate brand awareness and create, maintain and strengthen brand image, because strong brands that are trusted by customers produce strong profits. Brand metrics therefore are critical, in order to understand how successful a brand is and adapt brand strategy accordingly.

As we set out in section 1.2, brand equity, image and premium are important measures to keep track of. But this is challenging because brands are intangible. The different valuations produced by different brand valuation specialists for the same brand show just how subjective the process can be. However, it's not so much the absolute value of their brand that is important for marketers, but rather an understanding of the elements that make up that value, and how to build on those to create more value. Indeed, it is the 'evaluation' rather than 'valuation' that counts – all the diagnostic work that goes on to determine how healthy brands actually are. Companies can find, for example, that the brands they love don't deliver much return, but the brands they pay little attention to are potential goldmines. The old adage 'you manage what you measure' is as true in brand valuation as anywhere: you can unlock far greater value from your brands by managing them better. And, crucially, rather than being a snapshot, brand evaluation is an ongoing iterative process – you can use it to improve.

Brand valuation companies such as Interbrand and Brand Finance are a rich source of help on this brand evaluation. Reports from Mintel and other market research companies often contain brand personality and brand attitude data. The YouGov Brand Index, for example, produces a wealth of brand data, including: media metrics (including Adaware, word of mouth and Buzz), brand health metrics (including awareness, quality, value, impression, reputation, satisfaction and recommendation) and purchase funnel metrics (including consideration, purchase intent and current customers).

YouGov Profiles is a segmentation and media planning tool for brands and their agencies. It is powered by a connected data vault that holds over 190,000 data points collected from 275,000 YouGov members in the UK. It allows marketers to profile their target audience at a granular level across multichannel data sets. Areas include demographics and lifestyle, media consumption, brand usage and perceptions, online and mobile behaviour, attitudes and opinions and social media engagement.

See more on brand metrics in section 2.2.

Sales funnel data

The sales funnel is the pipeline for future customer acquisition. Visually, it looks like an inverted pyramid, and illustrates the steps in a sales process, from lead generation to a completed sale. The top of the sales funnel is the widest, representing the largest possible universe of prospective buyers. The number of potential customers decreases at each step in the sales process and this is represented by a progressively narrower funnel.

The sales funnel is often related to digital marketing, and its aim is to drive visitors to your website and persuade them to buy.

For more information on sales funnel metrics see Pombriant (2014).

And for examples of sales funnels, and how to make and use one, see:

https://www.smartdraw.com/sales-funnel/

See more on sales funnel data in section 1.2.

Integrated sales and marketing data

As we pointed out in section 1.3, replacing organisational silos with cross-functional matrices, and aligning everyone's objectives around a customer orientation, makes it easier to define a common set of metrics that everyone signs up to. Too many companies still have a silo mentality, with competing objectives, targets and budgets – a state of affairs not conducive to what should be the overarching organisational aim of satisfying customers at a profit.

This tension is particularly pronounced in the relationship between sales and marketing, as we pointed out earlier. The two used to be far more integrated than they are now – after The Institute of Marketing and Sales Management dropped the 'Sales Management' part in 1963 each side went off in its own direction. In smaller companies sales and marketing are much more integrated than they are in larger ones. But sales has always remained at the sharp end – close to customers and the market – while marketing has traditionally had a more strategic focus on the entire business. This false dichotomy has been thrown into sharp relief with the growth of online marketing: marketers these days regularly engage directly with customers in a way that would in the past have been limited to the sales function, and in social media marketers often carry out all the early stages of the sales cycle.

So nowhere is functional integration more important than between marketing and sales. US marketing guru Philip Kotler, in the 2011 Chartered Institute of Marketing White Paper Marketing and Sales Fusion (which we referred to earlier), said: "...there is no question that, when sales and marketing work well together, companies see substantial improvement on important performance metrics – sales cycles are shorter, market-entry costs go down, and the cost of sales is lower."

Alan Tapp, professor of marketing at the University of the West of England, says that everything improves with sales and marketing integration, from better information flows, through more accurate return on investment and cost benefit accounting, to more strategic direction setting. And there are benefits to other departments too, points out Holger Ernst (2010). For example, the different orientations of sales and marketing provide complementary information that informs the NPD process. Combining strategic marketing information and specific customer information "helps avoid niche solutions for an individual customer that, in turn, neglect the attractiveness of larger market segments or market trends or are not aligned with the firm's overall product portfolio."

Shared budgets and shared goals are an obvious precursor to shared metrics.

Madhani (2016) suggests that a simple way to document an interactive sales and marketing process is to develop a Process Flow Diagram – something that sales and marketing need to develop together. This establishes a communications or feedback loop in which marketing data flows from marketing to sales and back again, enhancing the customer value proposition. "When sales and marketing activities are closely co-ordinated, sales collects valuable customer-related information such as changing customer needs as well as information on new developments from competitors. This information can be analyzed by marketing to develop appropriate marketing strategy in terms of customized products and programs, which sales needs to translate into action by executing it for increasing value for customers. Thus, marketing through its market research and sales through its market intelligence and direct customer contact serve as repositories of crucial customer and competitive intelligence."

Madhani proposes a number of different frameworks that have the potential to create collaboration between sales and marketing that will result in new ways to create and deliver value to customers.

Primary and secondary research

Primary research, also known as field research, is carried out specifically to answer the questions raised in a market research brief. It includes surveys (postal, face to face, telephone and internet), depth interviews, focus groups, projective techniques, experiments and observations.

Secondary research, also referred to as desk research, involves investigating data that already exists. It may take the form of internal records, or reports that have been collated for another purpose. It is usually done before primary research, and is much cheaper and is typically less time consuming. However, because this data hasn't been gathered for the specific purpose marketers are now considering, it has limitations.

Information sourced through either secondary or primary techniques can be either qualitative or quantitative. And it may be gathered from internal or external sources.

Qualitative information can't be measured or expressed in numeric terms. It is useful to the marketer as it often explores people's feelings and opinions.

Quantitative information can be measured and expressed in numeric terms. For example, the percentage market share held, the number of customers buying our product in a certain month, or the number of sales calls made in a week.

Techniques for collecting primary data

Primary research techniques include the following.

Self-completion surveys – These are completed by the targeted individual respondent, to whom they are sent via email or post. Increasingly there are self-completion questionnaires on websites, but because the respondents answering the questions are self-selecting this limits the value of the response. This type of questionnaire is cheapest to administer as it doesn't require an interviewer, either on the phone or face to face. However, it is also the least likely to be completed, and so has the lowest response rate. This means that the end result can be based on an unrepresentative sample. The most effective self-completion surveys are usually those that require 'tick box' answers.

Surveys via interview – These can be face to face or over the telephone, structured, semi-structured, or unstructured. Structured surveys are fully constrained by the requirements of the questionnaire, which is usually of a 'tick box' nature. Semi-structured surveys use a questionnaire that has a combination of tick box and open-ended questions, allowing a degree of probing. Unstructured interviews are used to elicit qualitative data, and the interviewer usually just has a list of topics to discuss.

Surveys by interview have a higher response rate than postal or email surveys, and face-to-face surveys generally have a slightly better response rate than telephone surveys. Telephone surveys are quicker and more economical, but again there is a danger that they are an unrepresentative sample, as individuals with ex-directory numbers and those registered with the Telephone Preference Service can't be included.

Focus groups – These also produce valuable qualitative data, and are useful in that they provide the opportunity for an individual's comments to 'spark off' ideas and discussion from others in the group. The group is usually made up of eight to ten members, and the value of the data gathered depends on the selection of respondents and the competence of the group 'moderator', who needs to be carefully trained.

Observation – This technique is increasingly used in retail environments. It looks at shopping behaviour and is used to inform category management. Video cameras are often used, although 'headcounts' are still carried out by personal observers. This can be relatively expensive, but reports on shopping behaviour may be jointly commissioned, spreading the cost.

Mystery shopping – Mystery shopping programmes are usually run by external specialist agencies. They involve selecting 'customers' from a database who most closely match an organisation's current customer base. These researchers are asked to make a specific purchase or enquiry and report back in a structured way about their experience and how customer-facing employees dealt with them.

Experimentation –Test marketing is the most obvious form of experimentation, where, for example, a mini-launch of a new product may take place in a smaller, similar market to the intended one. This allows marketers to consider customers' responses to the product itself, and its promotion, without

Sources of secondary data on markets, customers and competitors include those in the table below. (Members should remember the resources they have on MyCIM.)

Government sources.	Governments produce statistics on many areas, including population censuses, family expenditure surveys, import/ export statistics, production statistics and social surveys.
Commercial market research reports.	Produced by organisations such as Mintel and Frost & Sullivan, these industry reports are based on panel surveys and provide information on consumer activity and business-to-business markets.
Trade and industry sources.	Trade and industry bodies publish directories and other industry statistics, plus member survey results.
Competitor data.	Reports and Accounts are available on corporate websites, as well as evidence of marketing activity and plans.
Online information sources.	Competitor websites, online databases.
Media sources.	Quality business newspapers (such as the *Financial Times*) and specialised trade press (*The Grocer*, for example).
Social media feeds and blogs.	Feeds from influential blogs can alert you to what's happening in the market, and tools such as 'mention' can send you an alert whenever you or a competitor is mentioned in social media.
Financial, geographic and demographic databases.	Economic reviews, country reports and population databases.
Internal databases and records – from store audits or scanned data, for example.	Data might include sales figures, call reports, CRM entries and financial reports.

Table 2.1 Sources of secondary data

Geodemographic research is another source of data. In the UK it is based on postcode geography, and groups together people with similar characteristics, and even attitudes, who live in the same area. A Classification of Residential Neighbourhoods (ACORN) and Mosaic were the pioneering systems. Other companies offer these services, but

ACORN and Mosaic can be examined at no cost at various websites such as Zoopla, which is designed for citizens to understand their local community.

ACORN and Mosaic offer detailed insights into an area, down to postcode level. ACORN, for example, divides the UK population into 62 types of household, and provides information on the type of people in a postcode area, including key demographic and lifestyle information such as typical life stage, occupation, income, savings, car ownership, types of insurance they hold, supermarkets they shop at, newspapers and magazines they read, music they listen to, hobbies, health indicators, holiday destinations and spending on different activities.

However, some companies find segmenting their market by psychological factors, including values and beliefs, provides more useful insights.

Major sources of external secondary data that include geodemographics are syndicated services where data is collected and distributed to interested parties. Some of the most important ones are search engine traffic, emerging fashions, user-panel analysis, shopping agents and archive systems. (Bradley, 2013, pp85-86) The topics covered are often much wider than the main purpose: for example, magazine reading surveys often look at internet use too. Because big surveys have many users, the methodologies are accepted and robust, therefore trustworthy. And because they are long established, most have trend data going back for over 20 years.

Integrated channel data

"In many ways, integrated marketing communication has reached another crossroads as technology and digital media bring about change on a level that challenges practitioners to integrate in new ways, similar to the early days of social media. Big data is fundamentally shifting how marketers collect, analyze and utilize data across functions and organizations." So wrote Rachael Post and Dawn Edmiston in *The International Journal of Integrated Marketing Communications* in Spring 2014.

Big data describes a new generation of technologies and architectures that are designed to capture and analyse information, economically, from very large volumes of data. While big data can lend companies competitive edge, it is not the data itself, but the insights to be gleaned from it, that are important. One way big data can help is with 'predictive analytics'. These calculate likely human behaviour based on large amounts of current and historic indicative data gathered from multiple sources created by 'data exhaust' – the digital trail of data that users leave behind as they move about the virtual and physical worlds. Amazon has used predictive analytics for years to suggest items customers might like to purchase.

As ever, organisational silos hamper the effective use of big data – and big data may even reinforce them, because different departments often fight for ownership of data and use different measurement techniques to analyse it.

According to Nichols (2013), most organisations already collect a broad range of data within customer service, finance, operations, sales and other functions as well as marketing, but for big data to be a truly effective tool there must be channels that allow such data to be shared across functions. Only then can organisations begin to model their businesses through the collection and analysis of data across critical categories including "market conditions, competitive activities, marketing actions, consumer response and business outcomes."

Analytics

Data and analytics go hand in hand. A survey in 2013 by the Economist Intelligence Unit revealed that executives believed the most necessary skill for a successful marketer these days is the ability to use data analysis to extract predictive findings from big data. Citing Dahlström and Edelman (2013), Post and Edmiston (2013) suggest that database tools, social media, data collection and mining of every customer contact with a brand in real-time or as quickly as possible will challenge organisations to integrate across functions to provide customers with seamless externally-facing solutions based on customer needs. In order to develop these new brand experiences, organisations will have to integrate internal and external skills and structures such as customer service, marketing, social media, measurement, outside vendors and so on. In 2012 Gartner estimated that within five years (i.e. by 2017) most CMOs will have a bigger technology budget than CIOs.

Despite the impact of big data on integrated marketing communications, marketers should not become dependent on big data to drive business strategies, and regard it instead as a tool to drive consumer insights. It should inform, rather than consume, marketing efforts. To extract maximum value out of big data and analytics, organisations need to invest in ensuring that their marketers have an understanding of both strategic planning and data analysis.

Dashboards

Marketing dashboards are graphical descriptions of data and information demonstrating performance and trends, which managers can use to inform strategic and operational decision making. We look in more detail at dashboards in Chapter 4.

Marketers can access dashboards either free or at low cost. One source is Google Analytics.

HOW DIFFERENT DATA SOURCES WORK TOGETHER TO HELP MARKETING ANALYSIS

Product and pricing metrics

These two key areas of marketing mix measurement are highly tangible and closely allied. Pricing metrics can be used in an integrated way to determine optimum prices for different elements of a product line or category.

Pricing basket metrics – Can show what products customers are buying together as a basket or bundle, and therefore which products lend themselves most obviously to being marketed on a bundled basis. They can also inform decisions on which other products to **cross-sell**, **discount** or **upsell** to the same customer:

- **Cross-selling** is when a customer chooses a product, and the system presents them with recommended related products to add to their purchase.
- **Upselling** is when customers choose a product, and the system presents them with recommended superior alternatives (normally with some incentive) to replace their original choice.

REAL LIFE

As far back as 2006, Amazon reported that 35% of its revenues accrued directly from cross-selling and upselling initiatives (Mulpuru, 2014). Amazon achieves this by using pricing metrics to **bundle sales** to the customer: the customer can add two or more recommended complementary products to their basket either from the product page or at checkout stage.

Amazon often sells price-bundled products such as books and CDs at a discount in order to increase the perceived value of multiple products bought at the same time.

Frequently Bought Together

Price for all three: $497.87

Add all three to Cart
Add all three to Wish List

☑ This item: Playstation 4 console by Sony Play station 4 **$399.00**
☑ Playstation 4 Dualshock 4 wireless controller by Sony Computer Entertainment Playstation 4 **$58.88**
☑ FIFA 14 - PlayStation 4 by Electronic Arts Playstaion 4 **$39.99**

Price elasticity metrics – Can help inform decisions on which products can sustain premium pricing strategies without the need for discounts. These metrics can be extended further into product **cross-elasticity measurement**. Here you can analyse different product price elasticities to identify how one product might be affected as a result of increasing or lowering the price of another in the same category.

Pricing benchmark measurements of competitor offerings – Can also be used to set the price of a product above, below or at par with the price of a similar competitor product.

Using pricing metrics to gauge how demand fluctuates between a set of products allows marketers to develop actionable strategies around product development, product categorisation, and bundling and portfolio development. This benefits both the customer and the organisation.

Brand metrics

The growth of both digital and offline tools for marketing analytics has afforded marketers greater access to a sophisticated range of brand metrics, all of which can have a significant impact on each other. You can easily measure key factors such as brand awareness, value and positioning both offline and online, and you can measure the impact on brand metrics of different campaigns and related activities on an integrated basis by combining a variety of different measurement tools.

The key issue for the marketer is to select the brand metrics and tools that are most relevant to measuring the brand objectives they have set, whether in the private, public or not-for-profit sector context. The onus is on the marketer to ensure that the brand metrics they use are relevant and responsive to changes in the environment, and that they underpin marketing efforts to grow brand awareness, brand loyalty and brand value.

Marketers need to apply brand metrics to meet objectives such as the following:

* Gauge how customers think and feel about the brand.
* Pinpoint changes in customer or market sentiment.
* Identify the extent of customer engagement.
* Benchmark against competing brands.
* Identify ways of enhancing brand positioning.

Key brand metrics that marketers seek to measure in order to meet such objectives, and which often have a clear impact on each other, include:

* Brand awareness.
* Brand recognition.

- Share of voice.
- Values associated with the brand.
- Advertising recall.
- Advertising response.
- Brand advocacy/loyalty.
- Competitor impact.
- Online brand presence.

REAL LIFE

The UK charity the Foundation for the Study of Infant Deaths (FSID) has for over 40 years taken a leading role in working to prevent Sudden Infant Death Syndrome (SIDS). In 2013 the charity relaunched under a new brand name, The Lullaby Trust, accompanied by a new colourful blue and yellow brand identity. The Lullaby Trust used and compared online and offline brand metrics to measure the impact of the new brand. A year after the relaunch metrics recorded the following results:

- A 274% increase in the number of orders for the charity's core information leaflet.
- An increase in mailings of bereavement support leaflets from 4,000 to 19,000.
- An increase from 2,000 to 9,000 rebranded thermometers sold to parents wanting to monitor the temperature of their baby's room.
- An increase in the number of calls to the charity's information and advice helpline and bereavement support helpline of 26% and 17% respectively.

Source: CharityComms, 2014.

Digital brand metrics are now used routinely by organisations in both the private and public sector. Westminster City Council, for example, runs a quarterly Reputation Tracker survey among a random sample of 500 residents to evaluate the impact of its communications activity. Such activities help marketers to develop an understanding of the relationship between core measurements of a brand's value and the way it is positioned in the target marketplace.

You can use a range of digital metrics to measure the effect of different brand activities. After a branding campaign, for example, you can use changes in the number of visitors to your organisation's website to begin to measure the campaign's success, and, in combination with other metrics, gauge its effectiveness through different media channels. Where are new visitors coming from, for example – display advertising, social media etc?

Furthermore, you could use digital tools such as those at Socialbakers to compare the change in brand positioning against key competitors, and map this against other online metrics to measure changes in the number of social media followers, increases in the number of sales leads or online subscriptions and so on.

You could then add Google Analytics to the portfolio of brand metrics to track changes in, say, share of search relative to competitors, in order to gauge whether the brand campaign has also had an impact on the level of 'share of online voice'.

Other online brand metrics that can have a strong positive impact on each other when used on an integrated basis include the examples in Fig 2.2.

Brand metric	Digital brand metric
Awareness	Page impressions Video views
Consideration	Time spent on site Community members Polls Competition entries Level of engagement
Favourability	Number of shares/likes Positive blog/social media coverage
Purchase	Sales
Loyalty	Referral

Fig 2.2 Integrating offline and online brand metrics

Examples of digital brand metrics tools that can be used to measure the relative impact of digital communication on an organisation's brand positioning might include:

- Twitalyzer to measure Tweets.
- Socialmention for measuring real-time conversations.
- Google Analytics and Doubleclick for measuring changes in brand sentiment over time.

Channel metrics and profitability
Marketers in a variety of different sectors are making increasing use of multi-channel marketing, with many organisations enhancing offline channel strategies with a range of digital marketing channels, including social media channels such as Pinterest, Instagram, Twitter and Facebook.

By analysing the relative impact of different offline and online channels on branding, sales and customer loyalty, for example, marketers can gain real insight into which channel activities deliver the greatest return on investment and other measures of value.

But to measure the impact of multi-channel marketing, marketers needs to make clear decisions about what to measure, and this will be related to the objectives they set for their marketing activities at the outset.

The most important measure could well be an evaluation of which channel or mix of channels would be likely to have the greatest impact on a specific marketing activity, and the likely contribution of each channel to the desired outcome. After all, given that marketers are increasingly having to demonstrate clear evidence to senior management that they have optimised marketing investment, they need an in-depth understanding of what drives effective marketing responses through each channel they use.

One obvious strategy, therefore, would be to measure and compare operational metrics across each marketing channel used for any specific activity.

Digital measurement tools such as Google Analytics and WebTrends can be effectively combined with offline tools such as mail response rates and advertising tracking to provide robust multi-channel measurement solutions and dashboard reports showing how the selected combination of marketing channels is performing for any marketing activity, such as a brand or advertising campaign.

This same approach and data enable the marketer to build an intuitive set of key performance indicators (KPIs), which are specific to the marketing activity and objectives under consideration.

For example, a marketer using a range of different channel platforms to drive customer traffic might want to use measurement tools such as:

- GetResponse to measure mail and email response rates.
- Google Analytics to monitor changes in visitors to the website.
- Google or IBM Analytics to track Facebook likes and Twitter re-tweets of the content generated for the traffic campaign.

By analysing the impact of such channel metrics on each other, marketers can generate effective operational metrics that can inform key objectives such as ability to achieve intended reach and frequency, increase in customer engagement, and the optimal combination of content and channels to drive traffic and/or exert the highest impact on sales growth.

ACTIVITY 7
Consider how the channels to market for a range of goods and
services have changed over the past ten years. Why did these
changes occur? Examples to consider include books, electrical
goods clothing, music and fresh vegetables.

Promotional and media metrics

When analysing the effectiveness of promotional and media metrics,
marketers need to draw on a relevant range of measurements in
order to gain insight into the overall impact and effectiveness of their
promotional or media campaigns and related activities.

Promotional and media activities usually benefit from setting metrics
that can be used both before and after a campaign, so that they can be
applied, both individually and in conjunction with each other, to identify
and measure the specific impact the campaign has had, separate from
other factors (or 'noise').

Key metrics used in an integrated way in promotion and media activity
include the following examples:

- **Reach** – The total number of different people or households
  exposed, at least once, to a medium during a given period. Reach
  should not be confused with the number of people who will be
  exposed to and consume the advertising, however. It is just the
  number of people who are exposed to the medium and therefore
  have an opportunity to see or hear the ad or commercial.
- **Frequency** – The average number of times a promotion or media
  activity will be shown to the target audience.
- **Impressions** – The number of exposures of a promotion, such as an
  advertisement, to the target audience.
- **Gross rating points (GRPs)** – The product of the percentage of the
  audience *reached* by an advertisement, times the *frequency* they
  see it in a given campaign, which can be summed up as: frequency
  × % reached.
- **Target rating points (TRPs)** – Quantify the gross rating points
  achieved by an advertisement or campaign among target market
  individuals within the larger population.
- **Cost per thousand (CPM)** – The cost to reach one thousand people
  or households via a given advertising outlet or medium.
- **Cost per point (CPP)** – The cost of buying one rating point, or 1% of
  the target population.

Metrics of reach and frequency can also be used in any promotional
activity undertaken in addition to or in combination with advertising –
for example, direct mail or email marketing.

For digital promotional and media activity, other metrics that can be used in conjunction with each other might include the following (and all of them can be utilised via website measurement software or tools such as Google Analytics).

- **Acquisition metrics**
  - Additional traffic acquired via the activity.
  - Relative success of different promotional keywords and/or content utilised.
  - Impact of customer acquisitions across earned, owned or paid-for media respectively.
- **Behavioural metrics**
  - Web pages or videos/rich media viewed by the customer as a result of the promotion.
  - Level of repeat visitors generated.
  - Click-through rates, conversion rates, blocking rates on, for example, display, banner, mobile, paid, search and social media advertisements.
  - Success of calls to action incorporated into the promotion.
- **Outcome metrics**
  - Success rate of desired promotional or media outcomes – for example, response to email sign-up requests, brochure downloads, product purchases or increases in brand awareness.

In both offline and online promotions and media planning, the marketer has to carefully consider the purpose of the activity and the role of each medium in achieving that purpose. They then have to establish an objective set of measures with which to monitor the activity, and these measures should be capable of identifying the success or failure of each activity's component media.

REAL LIFE

Every year for over 60 years, UK citizens have sat down to watch or listen to the Queen's Christmas Speech to the nation. However, since the late 1980s, television media ratings for the speech have almost halved, despite the BBC, ITV and Sky now sharing rights to the speech.

By combining television with radio and online ratings, however, broadcasters were able to gauge that rather than an absolute decline in viewers for the speech, the advent of YouTube and social media has resulted in a sharp increase in the number of viewers watching the speech online instead of via the television. This, as you can see in the graph overleaf, has resulted in consistent total viewing figures for the past ten or more years. By combining both online and offline ratings metrics, broadcasters are able to determine the relative impact of different media for the speech, and to plan promotional activity accordingly.

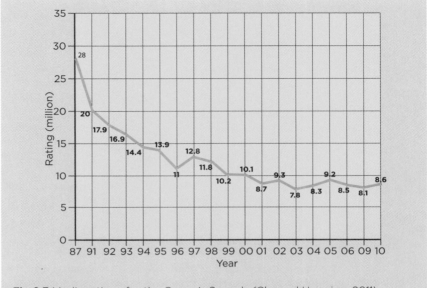

Fig 2.3 Media ratings for the Queen's Speech *(Channel Hopping, 2011)*

Service and satisfaction metrics

Marketers have measured customer service and satisfaction for many years in order to understand how to improve customer satisfaction, loyalty and customer lifetime value (CLV). But service and satisfaction metrics are not always compared and combined effectively enough to demonstrate the overall strategic impact of an organisation's customer-focused activity on satisfaction, loyalty or CLV.

As an example, a 2013 benchmarking study by Autotask showed that while 85% of organisations providing services ranked customer satisfaction as an important metric, only 10% claimed to be actively using customer satisfaction metrics, and only 9.5% ranked themselves as excellent at gathering customer data (Beard, 2013).

Key metrics that marketers can use in combination to gain real insight into customer service and satisfaction levels may include the following:

- Customer expectations of service versus perception of actual service received.
- Customer actual experience versus customer ideal experience.
- Customer likelihood to advocate or recommend the organisation to others.
- Customer intention to make repeat purchases from the organisation.
- Overall customer satisfaction.

Examples of measurement tools that marketers can use in conjunction with each other to gauge the relative impact of each strand of customer activity on satisfaction and loyalty might therefore include the following:

- Rating questions in customer surveys about satisfaction and advocacy.
- Helpline responses from contact details provided on websites, product packs or at the point of purchase.
- Customer follow-up outbound calling campaigns to measure satisfaction.
- Online merchant ratings of the organisation's product and service delivery.
- Online customer reviews of the organisation's products and services.
- Social media reviews about the organisation's products and services on sites such as Twitter and Facebook.
- Post-incident surveys (following recall of a defective product, for example) emailed to customers.

You can compare operational customer satisfaction metrics with each other to assess the impact of internal responsiveness to customer queries or complaints. Such metrics might include:

Volume and duration of calls/emails to customer contact centres/service teams.

- Rate of defects or recalls by volume across different product batches.
- Hold time and abandonment rates of customer service contact calls.
- Percentage of complaints resolved on the first contact versus those that are escalated.
- Overall rates of response to and resolution of customer complaints.

REAL LIFE

When a European telecommunications company wanted to lower the cost of its customer service operations it was concerned about potential loss of revenues from the very effective cross-selling done by its traditional call centres. When it investigated the options, the company realised that it could deliver 70% of existing customer-service contacts through digital solutions. By migrating part of its customer-service operations to similar 'digital-care programmes' the company lowered the cost of its customer service operations by around 30%, with no loss of revenue.

Source: Bianchi et al, *2014*

Customer loyalty and customer lifetime value (CLV) are often more strategic and long-term measures than customer satisfaction alone, so by combining these metrics marketers can measure the impact of both short-term customer satisfaction measures and more strategic longer-term relationship-building activities.

Metrics that can be used in combination for this purpose might therefore include:

- Customer defection or churn rates.
- Value of business lost through customer defection or churn.
- Cost of acquiring a new customer to replace a lost customer.
- Frequency with which customers refer the organisation to new prospects.

Financial and operational metrics

Most of the financial and operational metrics marketers use tend to fall into one of the following categories:

- **Cash flow metrics** – For example, net present value (NPV), return on investment (ROI), internal rate of return (IRR). These are used for evaluating investments and involve streams of cash flow over time.
- **Financial statement metrics** – For example, current ratio, inventory turnover, earnings per share.
- **Operational metrics** – For example, customer service metrics and supply chain management metrics.

Marketers shouldn't analyse these metrics in isolation from each other, but take an integrated approach in order to gain a strategic view of the impact of each set of metrics on the others. For example, operational metrics such as quality of delivery, purchase costs and supply chain process efficiency should be regularly monitored in conjunction with financial metrics around product costs, customer satisfaction and rate of returns. This allows marketers to anticipate and plan possible courses of action where product quality, profitability or customer satisfaction are shown to be potentially at risk through deteriorating supply-chain metrics.

Marketing metrics around an organisation's investments and resulting assets such as brands, customers and channels play a key role in determining a company's performance, shareholder and financial value, as Fig 2.4 (overleaf) shows.

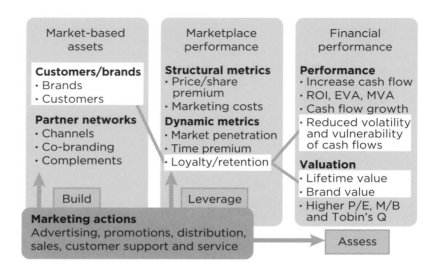

Fig 2.4 Linking market-based assets, market performance and financial performance *(University of Florida, 2004)*

ACTIVITY

Think back to a branding, advertising or other campaign or marketing activity that your organisation has implemented over the past 12 months. Answer the following questions:

How much planning and foresight was invested in planning measurement tools for the activity from the outset, and could this have been improved?

Was the activity measured in terms of its effectiveness and success on only one measure, or was a relevant range of metrics used for comparative analysis of the outcomes of the activity in question?

What types of combinations of measurement tools do you think the organisation could use more effectively in the future in order to better assess the relative impact of different media, channels, messages and other marketing elements on the overall campaign or marketing activity?

OVERCOMING THE CHALLENGES OF 'TOO MUCH' OR INCORRECT DATA

Given the wealth of different data sources available to marketers, including those listed above, it's not surprising that many organisations seem to be paralysed by data. Is there simply too much of it?

The Chartered Institute of Marketing addressed this issue in its 2009 White Paper *Measure for Measure*. In a section headed 'Balancing Metrics', it wrote:

"Whilst more widespread use of metrics across the board is to be welcomed, metrics usage brings its own issues and these need to be considered. Firstly, there are certain elements that are easier to measure (such as awareness), but which are of less importance when measuring the effects of marketing. Equally, there are some areas that are harder to measure, but more valuable in assessing marketing's value. As a result, marketing measurement can sometimes be skewed towards the elements that are measurable, rather than what needs to be measured. The focus on measuring the effects of communications campaigns is a result of this problem – it's an area that can be measured relatively easily, so there is more evidence of it being measured.

"To resolve this issue, a 'balanced scorecard' approach to metrics should be taken. The metrics should meet standard business criteria of being reliable, valid, responsive, clear and relevant. Secondly, whilst financial payback is important, financial metrics are not the only yardstick marketers should measure their business by. The metrics used should not be overly analytical; financial metrics are useful, but obsessive analysis is not. Again, a balanced approach helps prevent such distraction occurring.

"Thirdly, as the use of metrics is complex, there needs to be an emphasis on choosing and communicating a limited number of relevant metrics, rather than trying to do anything and everything. Finally, if it is suspected that the number and variety of metrics is stalling the process, create and implement a 'metric of metrics' – the balanced scorecard approach developed by Kaplan and Norton indicates how to achieve this. Provided the metric of metrics balances the individual measures, according to their observed contribution to effectiveness, it is unnecessary to worry unduly about the individual factors that constitute the score."

Clearly, we can get lost in metrics and therefore fail to obtain the results we need. It is all too easy to keep analysing, looking for more information and further justification rather than just making a decision based on the information we already have. It's worth bearing in mind the concept of statistical significance (covered below) here – provided the metrics are reporting something statistically significant that relates to objectives and strategies, you can make a decision around it. Checking the hypothesis is important, but once that's established it is decision time.

Another thing to bear in mind when using metrics is the value of effectiveness over efficiency. Metrics might be efficient, in that they measure well what they are intended to measure, but they could also be ineffective, in that they aren't providing useful results because they're measuring the wrong things. It goes back to the principle of 'doing the right things rather than doing things right'.

ACTIVITY 8
Look at how metrics are used in your organisation and identify the benefits and limitations of their use. If metrics are not currently used, what benefits could the organisation derive from using them?

Analysing different data sources

To make decisions, managers rely on accurate, timely and relevant information that is both comprehensive and succinct. Based on a clear identification of the data required, metrics information systems need to be devised to deliver this in a manner that is neither overly time-consuming nor expensive.

Good information systems are able to take the required information at the appropriate point as part of routine activity. For example, an important metric to most retail organisations is the number of visitors to their stores, and the best way to find this is to count people as they enter the store, rather than trying to derive it later from other information. Automated collection of data can be done through electronic counters across the entrance, and this will provide a reliable and consistent metric. Retailers such as Tesco have very sophisticated databases that record customer transactions in great detail, but such databases don't record the number of people who enter the store, browse and leave without purchasing, or those who don't participate in loyalty schemes such as the Tesco Clubcard. Electronic counters across entrances enable retailers to compare transaction data with footfall to establish the percentage of store visitors who make purchases.

Internal and external data sources – There is a balance to be struck between the amount of data collected, accuracy, cost and speed. You can always gather more data, in more detail and more quickly, but this comes at a price. Each data source, whether internal or external, needs to be checked for accuracy, reliability, cost, validity and so on. Internal data may be more readily available, and relatively cheap (the cost is typically the time it takes for someone to retrieve it), but if the data was collected for a different purpose (that is, nothing to do with marketing) it may be insufficiently reliable or accurate.

External data should be assessed against the same criteria. Secondary data may have been collected for a different purpose, which can undermine its validity, and even primary data may be inaccurate if the collection method was flawed.

Care also needs to be taken with all measures, internal and external, to ensure that the metrics aren't created purely because they are easy to measure – they have to measure the right things, even if that's more difficult. Similarly, when setting targets for improvement based on previous measures the target must be carefully analysed and worded to ensure that the basis of measurement is appropriate to the result. If measuring response time to emails, for example, a target could be set to reply to all customer email enquiries within 30 minutes rather than the average two hours. However, if an email response is sent to a customer after 26 minutes, but that response informs them that their email will be dealt with as soon as possible while the average time for a specific response is still two hours, the target may have been met, but the service to customers is unchanged. The target should be to provide resolution of the customer's enquiry within 30 minutes.

ACTIVITY 9

Create a table to analyse the credibility, reliability, validity and value of the data sources you currently use, or might potentially use, in your organisation.

Challenges presented by limited data analysis

According to the *2013 Marketing Analytics Benchmark Report* from Marketing Sherpa, 20% of marketers have very limited data or no data at all and just 14% have vast quantities of data. Some 40% reported having average amounts of data. This indicates that many marketers are working with limited data for analysis, and of those that do have data only 37% routinely and efficiently gain insight from it. Lack of resources and lack of time are the main reasons stated for not getting the insight, with lack of understanding about how to proceed being the third most common reason.

There is clearly a data gap. Even auditors and analysts find it difficult to get valid data in any sort of consistent format and it is, if anything, more difficult for everyone else. As marketing metrics data can be sourced from different systems and groups within the organisation, the collection process takes collaboration, co-operation and trust between the marketing analysts and the departments sourcing the required metrics and data. Again, this kind of 'seamless' working can be difficult to achieve.

To help overcome some of the challenges in collecting the right information, marketing needs to collaborate and co-operate with some of the other stakeholders to address the following issues:

- Set goals for collecting – The marketing data analyst must start with the simple but important question: "Are there data or metrics available for analysis to help with our planning and decision making?"
- Communicate – You need to ensure the stakeholders involved understand fully what data is required and when it is needed. The analyst needs to be sure the appropriate data will be available when they need it.
- Data organisation and formatting – When receiving data from a variety of sources you need tools to map, validate and cleanse it to ensure it is appropriate to use for marketing decision-making purposes.

Lack of data for social media analysis is a particular problem because, despite the plethora of data produced by digital marketing, it often can't answer marketers' most important questions. Some of the key challenges are as follows:

- The percentage of people who comment in social media is low, few comments in social media are about brands and services, and the comments there are don't typically cover the whole spread of experiences – people tend to comment on very good or bad experiences. This can leave large gaps in the information gathered.
- It can be difficult to attribute comments to specific segments – even identifying countries can be difficult, let alone regions. Breaking comments down further to customers or prospects, and particularly demographic factors like age and gender, can be almost impossible.
- The dynamic nature of social media makes it difficult to compare campaigns or activities – there may be factors this month that weren't relevant last month, for example. This can be due to changes in the number of people using social media, or changes in the way they use it, or because dramatic growth in the use of social media tools by marketers and PR teams is changing perceptions and conversations. The lack of consistency makes for limited information, which, in turn, affects the accuracy of social media measurements.
- Social media is very much about 'now', which makes it difficult for brands to use it to test adverts, new products and services, or almost any other future plan.

Statistical analysis
The Oxford Dictionaries define statistics as: "The practice or science of collecting and analysing numerical data in large quantities, especially for the purpose of inferring proportions in a whole from those in a representative sample." Statistics are very closely related to metrics as, in reality, the outputs of metrics are statistical in nature.

But the phrase attributed to 19th-century British Prime Minister Benjamin Disraeli – "There are three kinds of lies: lies, damned lies and statistics" – highlights one of the main problems with statistical analysis for strategic decision-making. Justifying an activity based on statistical analysis will often be greeted with mistrust because, it is argued, you can manipulate statistics to present the picture you want to present.

Statistical analysis is a mathematical method of interrogating data, and as such it is a component of data analytics. In relation to marketing metrics and business intelligence-gathering, statistical analysis involves collecting and interpreting data, and examining all the data elements in a set to look for linkages and correlations.

There are five steps in statistical analysis:

1. Describe the nature of the data to be analysed.
2. Explore the relationship between the data and the underlying population.
3. Create a model to summarise the relationship between the data and the underlying population.
4. Prove, or disprove, the validity of the model by means of the statistical analysis.
5. Develop predictive analysis for future scenarios to help guide future actions.

Overall, the goal of statistical analysis is to identify trends in order to make decisions about what to do in the future. Trends observed through statistical analysis can be used, for example, to create more appropriate levels of customer service, therefore increasing sales. The trend identified informs the decision-making process and therefore the outcomes to be included in strategy or tactics.

Statistical significance
Statistical significance is an essential element of 'statistical hypothesis testing', which is used to determine whether a 'null hypothesis' (that is, the general or default statement that nothing happened or changed) can be ruled out, and that our data is telling us that something has actually changed.

In any experiment or observation that involves drawing a sample from a population, there is always the possibility that an observed effect would have occurred due to sampling error alone. To determine if there really is a statistically significant difference between two statistics, or if it is simply 'chance', the key thing to look at is the size of the samples and determine the margin of error. For example, if you send out 180 emails, 90 with subject line A and 90 with subject line B, and observe an 'open rate' of 13.3% and 12.8% respectively, you really have no clue which one was better, because the relatively small sample means the margin of error is much bigger than the difference you measured here (that is, 0.5%). However, if you increased the sample size to 90,000 emails of each version and got the same open rates as before you could say that the first email *did* have an actual open rate that was higher than the open rate of the second email. This is because the large sample has reduced the maximum margin of error to significantly less than the difference you observed between A and B. To calculate the error margin – or the 'p value' as statisticians call it – and to establish if a change in your data measurements *is* statistically significant, you can use the original formulas for calculating this, but there are now many online calculators available to do this for you.

You can use statistical significance to look at a particular characteristic or a trend in order to see when either of them becomes statistically significant.

QUICK QUIZ – CHECK YOUR KNOWLEDGE

Questions
1. What do market-based assets include for an organisation?
2. What is the tool socialmention used for?
3. List some examples of cash-flow metrics.
4. According to the *2013 Marketing Analytics Benchmark Report* from Marketing Sherpa what percentage of marketers reported having very limited data or no data at all?
5. Which areas should be considered when building collaboration between the marketing function and other stakeholders to collect data?

Answers
1. Customers, brands, channels to market and the innovations of the organisation.
2. Measuring real-time conversations around the brand.
3. Net present value (NPV), return on investment (ROI), internal rate of return (IRR).
4. 20% of marketers reported having very limited data or no data at all.
5. Data organisation and formatting, setting goals for collecting, communicating.

BIBLIOGRAPHY

Anon (2009) Measure for measure: metrics and marketers in the NHS. *The Chartered Institute of Marketing.* https://www.cim.co.uk/media/4889/14264-nhs-paper-2.pdf

Anon (2013) *2013 Marketing Analytics Benchmark Report.* Marketing Sherpa. http://content.marketingsherpa.com/data/public/reports/benchmark-reports/EXCERPT-BMR-2013-Marketing-Analytics.pdf

Beard, R. (2013) *Customer satisfaction metrics: 6 metrics you need to be tracking.* Available at: http://blog.clientheartbeat.com/customer-satisfaction-metrics-6-metrics-you-need-to-be-tracking/

Bianchi, R., Schiavotto, D., Svoboda, D. (2014) *Why companies should care about e-care* McKinsey & Company. Available at: http://www.mckinsey.com/insights/marketing_sales/why_companies_should_care_about_ecare?cid=DigitalEdge-eml-alt-mip-mck-oth-1408

Bradley, N. (2013) *Marketing research: tools and techniques.* 3rd ed. Oxford, OUP.

Brinker, S. and McLellan, L. (2014) The rise of the chief marketing technologist. *Harvard Business Review,* Jul/Aug, Vol92(7/8), pp82-85.

Channel Hopping (2011) *The Queen's Christmas Speech: ratings from the last 20 years* http://channelhopping.onthebox.com/2011/12/22/the-queens-christmas-speech-ratings-from-the-last-20-years/

Charity Comms (2014) *The Lullaby Trust: a year after relaunch.* https://www.charitycomms.org.uk/the-lullaby-trust-a-year-after-relaunch

CIM (2011) *Sales and marketing fusion.* White Paper. http://www.cim.co.uk/files/msfusion.pdf

EIU (2013) Mind the Digital Gap. New York

https://www.cmo.com.au/article/464594/big_data_challenge_proves_key_obstacle_marketers/

Kaplan, R.S. and Norton, D.P. (1992) The balanced scorecard – measures that drive performance. *Harvard Business Review,* Jan/Feb, Vol70(1), pp71-79.

Madhani, P.M. (2016) Sales and marketing integration: enhancing competitive advantages. *IUP Journal of Business Strategy*, Dec, Vol13(4), pp50-77.

Mulpuru, S. (2014) *How to boost ecommerce sales with upselling.* https://conversionxl.com/blog/upselling-techniques/#

Nichols, W. (2013) Advertising analytics 2.0. *Harvard Business Review,* March, Vol91(3), pp60-68.

Pombriant, D. (2014) Data drives metrics. *CRM Magazine*, Jan, Vol18(1), p4.

Post, R. and Edmiston, D. (2014) Challenging big data preconceptions: new ways of thinking about data and integrated marketing communications. *International Journal of Integrated Marketing Communications,* Spring, Vol6(1), pp18-24.

University of Florida (2004) *Metrics for linking marketing to financial performance* http://bear.warrington.ufl.edu/CENTERS/MKS/invited/Metrics%20for%20Linking%20Marketing%20to%20Financial%20Performance.pdf

ACORN – www.acorn.caci.co.uk

Mosaic – www.experian.co.uk/marketing-services/products/mosaic-uk.html

Smart Draw – www.smartdraw.com/sales-funnel/

Zoopla – www.zoopla.co.uk

3.0
DIFFERENT MEASUREMENT TECHNIQUES

OUTLINE

This chapter explains the significance of different measurement techniques across a range of market contexts, including sector and lifecycle stage, among others. At the end of this chapter you will be able to:

- Identify the different types of measurement techniques.
- Outline and analyse metrics associated with brand, margins, profits, sales and business results.
- Understand different metrics for brand management, sales and business results.

3.1 IDENTIFY THE DIFFERENT TYPES OF MEASUREMENT TECHNIQUES

Companies at all lifestyle stages will need to use a mix of different metrics, including business-value metrics, strategic metrics, operational metrics, activity metrics, outcome-based metrics, leading indicators and predictive metrics. We provide a summary of these below.

Business-value metrics

Metrics that drive value for the business are influenced by marketing in three main areas:

- **Market-based assets** – These can include customers, brands, channels to market and innovations. Such assets may have intrinsic value, but when used in conjunction with other marketing activities they deliver greater value. For example, you might utilise an established brand to enhance the reputation of a new innovation.
- **Marketing capabilities** – To deploy resources efficiently and effectively within the marketplace the organisation needs a market orientation, which involves all areas of the organisation working together towards the goal of maximising customer satisfaction and profitability.
- **Marketing actions** – This involves using marketing assets and capabilities to help drive strategy.

McDonald (2006) defines the financial value that marketing can deliver as 'the application of marketing due diligence'. He proposes the following calculation for the shareholder value that you would expect to create through a proposed marketing strategy:

$$\text{Shareholder value} = \text{Probability adjusted cash flows expected from marketing activity} - \text{Value of capital employed} \times \text{Required rate of return} - \text{Potential loss from capital at risk}$$

Fig 3.1 Shareholder value calculation (*Source: McDonald, 2006*)

Strategic metrics

At a strategic level there are many areas that an organisation should measure. As strategy is a long-term view of where the organisation is, where it wants to go and how it will get there, the main issue to think about is the revenue-generating activities it can become involved in. At a strategic level the main metrics to consider are:

- Market share and relative market share.
- Market growth.
- Market demand.
- Market penetration.

The information for these metrics comes largely from research, both internal and external, and from primary and secondary sources. Market research reports from Mintel, Frost & Sullivan and others may be required to understand the total market value from which to determine market share. Industry journals can be helpful for market growth and demand levels.

Operational and tactical metrics

The main operational marketing metrics are related to the efficiency and effectiveness of marketing activities, including how much they cost and the return on investment in them. Efficiency measures the way an activity (either operational or tactical) is carried out to see if it was done as well as possible. Effectiveness measures whether the right thing was done and the result was the one intended. Put simply, efficiency is doing things right while effectiveness is doing the right thing. Marketers can use a whole array of metrics to measure the effectiveness and efficiency of the marketing mix elements. We detailed these in Chapter 1, but will briefly reprise them here.

Product
- Marketing cost per unit.
- New product adoption rate, percentage of new products.
- Cannibalisation rates.

Price
- Sales price variation.
- Profit impact.
- Price premium.
- Price elasticity of demand.

Promotion
- Share of voice.
- Recall, recognition.
- Response rate.
- Conversion rate.
- Redemption rates.
- Reach.

Online
- Page impressions.
- Total clicks.
- Cost per action.
- Cost per lead.
- Social media activity.
- Bounce rates.
- Downloads.

Place/distribution
- Average transaction value.
- Average transaction volume.

- Inventory turnover.
- Sales per square foot.

Activity metrics
These essentially involve counting and reporting. Examples include the number of leads generated at a trade show, or tracking downloads from, or the number of visitors to, a website. These measures are limited in that on their own they rarely demonstrate the contribution marketing makes to business outcomes.

Outcome-based metrics
These link marketing metrics to organisation strategy. Examples include **market share**, **customer value** and **new product adoption**. For example if your objective is to achieve a 20% share of the real-fruit smoothie market within two years, you have to develop a strategy to achieve this, using the full marketing mix and utilising major supermarket chains as the channel. The metric for this outcome-based objective would have to focus on the share of market achieved as a result of the marketing mix actions.

Leading indicators and predictive metrics
Many metrics focus on measuring what has happened. Leading indicators are measures of potential future activity or trends that help you decide on your future direction. They depend on sufficient historical information to be able to predict for the future. As an example, if you were seeking to increase your share of customer (that is, getting customers to spend more with you) then a metric such as **customer lifetime value** (explained in section 3.2) could serve as a leading indicator to measure whether the organisation is achieving its objective.

A good metric for leading indicators is a **causal forecast**. This is an estimating technique that assumes that the variable to be forecast (the 'dependent variable') has a cause-and-effect relationship with one or more other variables ('independent variables').

ACTIVITY 10

Based on the current lifecycle phase of your organisation, and assuming current trading information is available, nominate the metrics that might be most appropriate for you, as the marketing manager, to use to create a business plan, and explain why. In addition, consider what further information you might need to develop additional metrics, and how you could obtain this information, taking into account whether the benefits you would get would justify the cost involved in collecting the data. If required by your management, how would you calculate the cost/benefit ratio and justify the expenditure for information gathering?

Brand metrics

Much has been written on the subject of metrics for brands and
brand management, but a major issue is that there is no uniformly
applied definition of the term 'brand'. Brand means different things to
different people. According to Haigh, cited in McDonald and Mouncey
(2009), there are three concepts that are sometimes referred to as
the brand:

- **A logo and associated visual elements** – These are often
  legally protectable elements that are used to differentiate one
  organisation's products from another. To have value these symbols
  need to carry 'goodwill', which is acquired by providing high-quality
  products and by giving good service over a long period.
- **A larger bundle of trademarks and associated intellectual property
  rights** – These can include domain names, product design rights,
  packaging, copyrights in associated colours and other elements
  used within marketing promotional materials.
- **A holistic company or organisational brand** – A combination of all
  the legal rights in addition to the culture, people and programmes
  of an organisation provides a basis for differentiation and value
  creation. Overall this represents the value proposition that creates
  stronger customer relationships.

If people can't even agree on what a brand is, then defining brand
equity is even more of a challenge. It has been defined by MacInnis and
Park, cited in Davis (2013) as "the financial value of a brand, reflecting
its efficiency in attracting and retaining customers." But what about
the brand equity measures? Ambler (2003) recognises that to measure
brand equity some basic questions have to be answered:

- Are potential customers aware of the brand?
- What proportion of the intended market has bought the brand?
- How do they rate the brand's quality?
- How satisfied are they with their experience of the brand?
- Do they have the brand habit – that is, are they loyal?
- How easy is it to locate the brand?

Further, Ambler defines general brand equity metrics. See Fig 3.2
(overleaf).

Consumer metric	Measured by
Familiarity	Salience – that is, familiarity relative to the other brands in the consideration set.
Penetration	Number of customers or the number of active customers as a percentage of the intended market.
What they think about the brand	Brand preference as a percentage of preference of other brands within the consideration set, or intention to buy, or brand knowledge.
What they feel about the brand	Customer satisfaction as a percentage average for the consideration set.
Loyalty	This may be behavioural (share of category requirements, repeat buying, retention, churn) and/or intermediate (commitment, engagement or bonding).
Availability	Distribution – for example, weighted average percentage of retail outlets carrying the brand.

Fig 3.2 Brand equity metrics *(Source: Ambler, 2003)*

Sales force and sales funnel metrics – Many organisations, especially in a business-to business-environment, use a sales force as part of their sales operations. Measuring the effectiveness of the sales force is important and you could use a number of different metrics to do this. You could measure, for example:

- Numbers of calls.
- Number of contacts made.
- Potential accounts.
- Active accounts.
- Net sales contribution.
- Average sales per call.

You would usually measure sales performance against historical data, using the historic sales as a baseline. You can make adjustments to cover the long-term effects similar to the 'continuing operations' comparisons mentioned above.

For sales funnel metrics, see Chapter 1.

Customer lifetime value (CLV) is a forward-looking indicator that forecasts the value of the relationship between an organisation and a customer and how much profit the organisation will make out of that customer. Farris et al (2010) define it as: "The present value of the future cash flows attributed to the customer relationship." In essence, what this metric demonstrates is how much a customer is worth to the organisation expressed as a lump sum in current money terms. It helps an organisation to decide which customers are worth the most, based not on historical data, but on potential future income.

A simple metric formula used frequently by marketers to calculate CLV works as follows:

(average value of a sale) x (number of repeat transactions) x (average retention time in months or years for a typical customer).

For example, if a typical supermarket customer spends £100 each time they visit, and visit once a week for 45 weeks of the year (allowing for holidays and other time away from home) their annual spend is £100 x 45 = £4,500. If we now assume that a customer remains loyal to a supermarket for ten years this would give a CLV of £45,000 (£4,500 x 10).

This is a 'quick and dirty' calculation since a true CLV should discount future sales (or better still profits) to their 'net present value', but the relative value of each customer broadly holds using this method.

ACTIVITY 11

Consider the concept of customer lifetime value in the context of you as the consumer. Which company would you describe yourself as a loyal customer of and how might your interactions with that organisation increase your value to them? Do you think you sometimes spend more than you intend to with them? How would you set about calculating your likely lifetime value to that organisation?

Communications metrics

The Barcelona Principles are the first international framework for measuring communications performance. First introduced in 2010 by AMEC (the International Association for the Measurement and Evaluation of Communication), they were revised in 2015 to reflect changes in the media landscape and the emergence of integrated communications.

To see the Principles, and the main changes, see:
https://amecorg.com/barcelona-principles-2-0-infographic/

Portfolio management

There are a number of traditional models that you could use to measure the success of your company's product or service portfolio, ranging from the product lifecycle (introduction, growth, maturity, decline) through the Boston Consulting Group (BCG) Matrix, to more involved models for understanding investment in particular areas, such as the GE Matrix.

We will cover measures needed for the start-up, growth and maturity stages of the product lifecycle in section 4.1. Understanding the lifecycle stage of products helps to inform decisions regarding marketing activity and investment, as well as establishing the need for new product development. Relevant measures might include:

- Number of new products introduced in a given time period.
- Revenue from new products – typically expressed as a percentage of total sales.
- Margin on new products.

The best known and longest-established portfolio appraisal tool is the BCG Matrix. The matrix has two axes – relative market share on the horizontal (x) axis and market growth on the vertical (y) axis. A company's portfolio of products or services can be positioned across the two-dimensional field this creates, based on their scores on each dimension. Traditionally the quadrants of the matrix provide a guide as to the appropriate resource investment strategy for each product that falls within them. These range from 'stars' in the top left quadrant – those with high share in high-growth markets – to 'dogs' in the bottom right quadrant – those with poor relative market share in declining markets.

Relative market share is a more complex idea than simple or absolute market share. It is based on the principle that the biggest supplier to a market is likely to be further up the experience curve than any of its competitors and therefore likely to be a lower-cost operator with more resources to bring to a competitive fight. Your product's relative market share is its absolute share divided by that of its biggest competitor. So, for example, a 20% share can put you high on the x axis if the next best operator has a 5% market share (making your relative share 4.0). In another market though, a 20% share might make you a dog because the biggest player there has a 60% absolute share (giving you a relative share of 0.33). The midpoint on the x axis is 1.0.

The criteria for defining the markets that the products are operating in have to be clearly defined at the outset in order to provide meaningful data and avoid expensive mistakes.

Return on investment (ROI)

This is a measure of how well assets are being used. In simple terms it relates profits to capital invested. In a marketing context, ROI is often used to set targets for and then measure the return gained on a marketing expenditure investment in a particular marketing activity, over a comparatively short time frame. More generally ROI measures returns on capital invested over longer periods, either the historic record of a company or a product or service, or the projected returns of a proposed investment over a defined number of years. For marketing-inspired capital investments, such as new product development, a major rebranding or a new website, the measurement of the return achieved will also be long term.

When discussing ROI for marketing expenditure, measures may relate simply to the cash profit return after deducting the cost of the activity – so return minus investment. More generally the ROI measure tends to be calculated as return divided by investment, expressed as a percentage.

The marketing ROI measure is most useful for comparing different potential uses of the marketing budget – you can forecast which activity is likely to yield the highest return. You can also use ROI to measure the effect of activities post implementation, to provide lessons for future planning – provided you measure the results accurately.

CASE STUDY

ROI and pipeline measurement
In 2011 Brendan Dineen, director of demand programmes for the UK and Ireland at blue-chip company IBM, talked to *The Marketer* about why he wanted B2B marketers to start talking about ROI and the importance of using metrics to evaluate business lead generation. Dineen's job is to drum up business leads or, in other words, populate the sales pipeline.

"I'm at the gritty end of marketing," he told *The Marketer*. "I work with lots of colleagues who are responsible for other elements of the marketing mix, from communications to marketing planning, advertising and market intelligence. My job is to turn all of that into the cold hard facts of business opportunity."

His team is split into five different areas covering the company's different markets, and the team's role overall is to identify "millions of dollars-worth of pipeline," he said. Then, critically, they have to look at how much of that pipeline turns into revenue for IBM. "I'll ask my team how much they spent, and then we'll run it through the acid test of ROI," said Dineen, who described his task as "trying to use facts to manage the business."

As any marketer knows, facts can be hard to pin down in a discipline that relies largely on emotions for the effectiveness of campaigns. But Dineen is ruthlessly committed to metrics: "When I speak to the heads of each of my teams at 10 o'clock every Monday morning my questions are all very simple. I want to know how many responses we have generated so far this year, how many we planned to, how many of those we have filtered into something we would want to further qualify and how many are not worth progressing at this point. Then I'll ask the leads people what is the value of the pipeline we've generated this year against what we planned. If it's better than we planned then we need to do more of it; if it's not, then we need to understand why."

Dineen thinks marketing spends too little time talking about ROI, and is trying to foster more discussion about the subject with industry colleagues. He believes more discussion would lead to more knowledge and greater understanding among marketers about the drivers of ROI, which would benefit business generally and marketers specifically. As he pointed out: "If we can understand and compare and feel comfortable with the value of brands relative to one another, surely we must be able to do the same with ROI."

Source: Barda, T. (2011)

QUICK QUIZ – CHECK YOUR KNOWLEDGE
Questions
1. What does customer lifetime value demonstrate?
2. What are the three concepts that make up the brand according to McDonald and Mouncey?
3. Why were the Barcelona Principles updated in 2010?

Answers
1. Customer lifetime value demonstrates how much a customer is worth to the organisation expressed as a lump sum in current money terms.
2. The logo (visual element), trademarks (including IP rights) and a holistic company.
3. To reflect changes in media landscape and the emergence of integrated communications.

BIBLIOGRAPHY
Ambler, T. (2003) *Marketing and the bottom line*. Harlow, Prentice Hall.

Ambler, T. and Roberts, J.H. (2008) Assessing marketing performance. Don't settle for a silver metric. *Journal of Marketing Management*, Vol24(7/8), pp733-750.

Barcelona Principles 2.0 – https://amecorg.com/barcelona-principles-2-0-infographic/

Barda, T. (2011) Pumping up the pipe line. *The Marketer,* March, pp22-27.

McDonald, M and Mouncey, P. (2009) *Marketing accountability: a new metrics model to measure marketing effectiveness.* London, Kogan Page.

Davis, J.A. (2013) *Measuring marketing: 110+ key metrics every marketer needs.* 2nd edition. Chichester, John Wiley.

Farris, P.W., Bendle, N.T., Pfeifer, P.E. and Reibstein, D.J. (2017) *Key marketing metrics: the 50+ metrics every manager needs to know.* 2nd ed. Harlow, Pearson.

4.0
CHOOSING THE RIGHT METRICS AT THE RIGHT TIME

OUTLINE

Different metrics are required at different points in a company's lifestage so choosing the right metric is important. At the end of this chapter you will be able to:

- Understand how to choose the right metric and the right time.
- Understand what is an appropriate measure.
- Begin to build your management reporting requirements.
- Understand how to create and use metrics-based dashboards.

101

METRICS AND ORGANISATIONAL LIFECYCLE STAGE

Organisations face different challenges at different stages of their lifecycle and the metrics they employ at each stage have to reflect these.

Start-up companies

Every start-up organisation has limited resources, whether people, money or time. In the short term, while growth may be desirable, companies need to understand their limitations and metrics can help them to identify where they should allocate their limited financial resources to get the best return. According to C&M Consulting Group (2014) young organisations have a hard time understanding what to track to ensure they grow at an optimum rate. C&M says there are three scoring grades ('good', 'okay' and 'bad') to be awarded on three factors – cash burn, customer acquisition and product development.

1. Cash-burn rate – This is a measure of how soon it will be, at current expenditure rates, before the available cash runs out. The reason businesses raise money from external sources is to buy time to extend their cash-burn rate. As an overall business metric, watching cash is very important in order to understand how long the organisation can continue to fund its activities. As a guide, over 12 months of cash provides safety, while organisations with less than three months of cash are in the danger zone and need to reduce expenditure or look for additional finance by generating profits or raising new investment funds.

2. Customer acquisition/growth rate – This measures the conversion of enquiries into paying customers. A start-up company will take some time to build this metric, but it should measure it on a month-by-month basis. It isn't just the acquisition rate that's important, however. You also need to understand what is driving increases in the rate – like the size and nature of the 'sales funnel', which is the pipeline for future customer acquisition (discussed later in the chapter). So, for example, if digital marketing is a key tool for the organisation, then social media interaction could give a good indication of the likely future acquisition rate – more interaction now may mean more customers in two months' time.

3. Product development response – Start-up organisations, by their very nature, have relatively new and untried products or services. The 'product development response' is the speed at which areas of the product or service (including the process used to serve customers) that are not as good as they should be, are rectified or turned round. Product response rate is not a typical metric, but for start-ups it can be critical because it allows them to ensure customers are satisfied from the outset.

A major challenge for start-up businesses is the lack of historic data against which to compare current performance. Metrics are being created and used for the first time, or at best being assessed against the predictions in the original business plan. This doesn't undermine the value of metrics during the start-up phase though. Their initial use will at least create benchmarks for the future. But most initial metrics will be estimates based on research from relevant sources, with the specific information required depending on the sector the company operates in, the scale of the organisation and its ambition in the early phases.

Sources of information to inform metrics at the start-up stage include:

• Awareness factors.
• Customer advocacy factors.
• Responses to promotional offers.
• How the product or service is used.

These will inform subsequent 'hard' data metrics like:

• New customer gains.
• Customer acquisition costs.
• Cost per lead.
• New product purchase rate.
• Activity ratio for social media.

Developing companies
During the development stage, an organisation's challenges change from gaining customers to retaining them while at the same time driving and maintaining growth rates.

You need to consider **growth rates** carefully, because changes in the organisation and its trading environment over time make it difficult to compare like with like. For example, as an organisation grows it may take on more sales staff and increase the number of outlets it sells through. This in itself implies the organisation has grown, but you need to check growth in each of those outlets too. You can use 'continuing operations' measures to do this. For example, if a retail chain is growing and now has 12 outlets compared with just eight six months ago, you would compare how those eight outlets performed then against how they are performing today, as well as measuring the performance of the *total* business today. Often, on the business news, you will hear major retailers' annual performance being described as the percentage growth in 'continuing stores', which means comparing the performance of stores that were trading this time last year against their performance this year.

Developing businesses also need to consider the **compound annual growth rate**, which provides an indication of the growth performance of the organisation. This is the smoothed annualised growth over a specified period of time. For example, if a business grew by 30% in its first year and then saw no growth for the next two years, its compound annual growth rate would not be 10% – that would require 33.1% growth over the three-year period.

Specific areas of interest to inform metrics in the development stage are:

- Areas generating growth.
- Triggers of growth.
- Factors that influence customers' views.
- Media outlets capable of providing most potential new business.

Mature companies

As companies reach the maturity stage their sales tend to flatten or even decline. They can't sustain the growth rates of their earlier phases, so they may need different metrics to reflect market changes. Maintaining maturity and staving off the 'decline' phase for as long as possible is often the target, and metrics should reflect this. So, for example, they may need to think harder about introducing new products, but they also need to be alert to the danger of cannibalisation, and using the **cannibalisation rate** metric discussed in Chapter 1 should help them determine the optimum time to introduce the new product – soon enough to beat competitors but late enough to minimise the effect on existing products.

Other information areas to consider in the maturity phase are:

- Trends and preferences for the product offered.
- Brand advocates and influencers for the product.
- Other products customers show interest in.
- Competitor activity in similar product areas.

CHOOSING APPROPRIATE MEASURES TO IMPROVE MARKETING PERFORMANCE

As we have seen so far in this book, you can measure many areas through analytics (the tools and methods of analysis, which produce the metrics to inform decision-making). But you have to ensure you use the appropriate measures if you wish to add value to the organisation. The problem is, views differ as to what the 'appropriate' measures are. Ambler (2003) cites examples of contrasting advice from senior executives in leading organisations:

- The general approach – using a few metrics that can be applied in every organisation. However, Ambler found that while many senior managers stated that they could name the five metrics most important to them, there was little consistency to the metrics they selected.
- The tailored approach – choosing metrics based on what the organisation is specifically trying to achieve.

Clearly, you need to do some analysis in order to determine the most appropriate analytics for any given situation. But the tailored approach is probably advisable so that you can address specific questions from key stakeholders. You may need to use a wide variety of metrics initially, and then study the results from them to determine which provide the most salient data to inform the setting and monitoring of key performance indicators.

Integrating data sources, including big data sets

While finance is generally agreed to be the language of business, there is growing recognition of the importance of non-financial metrics. Ambler and Roberts (2008) cite research that demonstrates this, particularly in situations where non-financial performance indicators predict future cash flow. The combination of financial and non-financial data can be powerful.

Similarly, while much has been written recently about the amount of information that can be obtained through digital marketing analytics, the data from both on- and offline sources needs to be combined to provide a fuller picture. A marketing information system (MKIS) should integrate data from all of the organisation's customer data sources to enable informed business decisions and to facilitate better management of customer relationships. When data is integrated marketers benefit from better customer insights, which lead to higher conversion rates, improved retention rates and better customer service.

The most important integration required, however, is that of metrics with strategies and objectives, so that all stakeholders can see the link between the marketing data and their own involvement in the organisation.

We discussed 'big data' in section 2.1. Gartner defines big data as: "high volume, high velocity, and/or high variety information assets that require new forms of processing to enable enhanced decision-making, insight discovery and process optimisation." In the commercial world, recent developments in computing power make it possible to capture and correlate bigger and bigger data sets in a bid to derive fresh insights. Companies such as Amazon and eBay have millions of customers worldwide, for example, and interactions with them generate vast amounts of data. An article by IDC (2014) suggested that the volume of business data worldwide doubles in size every two years, and by 2020 the digital universe will reach 44 zettabytes, or 44 trillion gigabytes.

This level of information, in theory at least, enables marketers to gain insights into any aspect of customer buying behaviour, whether pre- or post-purchase, and to make informed decisions based on them. But the metrics drawn from the analysis of 'big data' should be integrated with other, more traditional data sources in order to add all-important context.

With so much data available, there is also a danger that we spend too much time analysing it and too little time making decisions based on it. Focusing too much on capturing data without considering how to use it to improve marketing results is a trap organisations of all sizes can fall into. But collecting data for collection's sake is not good business practice, and you need to strike a balance to avoid analysis paralysis.

We mentioned the importance of effective team structures in being able to use marketing metrics in section 1.3, along with the importance of finding a common set of metrics aimed at 'satisfying customers at a profit' that everyone can buy into. Matrices are one tool for doing this. Another is the balanced scorecard.

Using and developing balanced scorecards for marketing

The balanced scorecard was developed by Kaplan and Norton in 1992 to help organisations to set objectives that bring together the perspectives of a variety of different stakeholders and to link those objectives directly to the evaluation of performance. A useful definition runs as follows:

"The balanced scorecard is a strategic planning and management system that is used extensively in business and industry, government and non-profit organisations worldwide to align business activities to the vision and strategy of the organisation, improve internal and external communications, and monitor organisation performance against strategic goals." (www.balancedscorecard.org)

The implication for marketers is that they have to balance their focus on marketing objectives with the overall goals of the organisation. Equally, the organisation is forced to integrate the customer perspective into its overall thinking.

The balanced scorecard suggests that an organisation should view itself from four different perspectives:

- **Innovation and learning** – Its ability to do both.
- **Internal perspective** – The factors that lead to customer satisfaction, such as employee attitudes and performance.
- **Customer perspective** – Customers' views are critical, and quality and customer service are paramount.
- **Financial perspective** – The organisation's financial performance.

This management system provides a key link between setting objectives and measuring performance, and balances activities across the organisation so that you can measure the effect an action in one area has on other functions. It encourages managers to cascade strategy through the whole of the organisation's processes and to rethink the way they do business. It offers the opportunity to link strategy with the structure of the organisation and, from a metrics perspective, demonstrates a clear link between strategy and the actions to be taken with the results expected and achieved.

The balanced scorecard covers the following measures:

- **Financial measures** – Typically include:
  - Revenue growth – sales and market share, new pricing strategies etc.
  - Cost management – revenue per employee, unit cost reductions etc.
  - Asset utilisation – inventory levels, return on capital etc.
- **Customer measures** – Should be set around the market segments the organisation is already serving or wants to serve, and include:
  - Market share – percentage of segment, percentage of the customer's total requirement.
  - Customer retention – defections, increase in sales to each customer, order frequency etc.
  - Customer acquisition – new customers, sales:enquiry ratio, order sizes etc.
  - Customer satisfaction – numbers of complaints, numbers of thanks etc.
  - Customer profitability – profit per customer, cost per transaction.
- **Internal business process measures** – Include:
  - Design – time to market, break-even time.
  - Build – numbers of defects, process time.
  - Delivery – percentage of on-time delivery, delivery time, stock-outs.
  - Service – satisfaction rating, customer re-orders.

- **Learning and growing measures** – Relate to the infrastructure the organisation needs in order to achieve its other objectives, and may include:
  - Employee capabilities – staff turnover, productivity, number qualified.
  - Information technology – customer information available, return on data.
  - Motivation and alignment – suggestions received and implemented, rewards provided.

These are all 'top level' measures, and within any area you can drill down into more operational and tactical detail.

Management reporting

Different reporting is required for different stages of the business planning and implementation cycle. Managers don't want to be bombarded with data and information but they do want to be kept informed. Hemann and Burbary (2013) identify the potential measurement frequencies for digital analytics programmes, and these can be translated to wider marketing metrics. See Fig 4.1.

Annual	Business and communications planning, long-range strategy, KPI assessment, goal setting.
Quarterly	KPI executive reviews, strategy shifts, problem escalation, cross-discipline interaction.
Monthly	KPI trends and insights, strategy evaluation, programme optimisation, problem resolution.
Daily	Media flow, news synopsis, top-line opinions.
Hourly	Competitive alerts and crisis management.

Fig 4.1 Reporting frequency *(Hemann and Burbary, 2013)*

Building metrics hierarchies and tracking interactions

As we've seen, metrics exist at different levels and marketers need to build a hierarchy to develop a full understanding of any situation. Hierarchies can be developed from the top down or from the bottom up:

- **Top down** – You decide on the strategic metric and then break this down into component parts, initially at an operational level and then at a tactical level, in order to be able to explore some of the more precise areas that feed into the top-level metric.
- **Bottom up** – You assign a metric to each individual area that can be measured, tactical and operational, and then group these together to develop the next level of measure to be applied, and so on, to arrive at a strategic metric.

Whether bottom up or top down, the elements of the hierarchy have to be fully linked and clear justification provided both for the inclusion of each individual element and for the way they build together.

When using metrics to measure marketing mix elements, you have to also consider and measure the way different factors interact with each other, because you could be making simultaneous changes in various areas of the mix. For example, a price promotion may require some advertising (or just emails to existing customers) to ensure customers are aware of it. You have to integrate all these factors into the overall metrics to determine which element had the biggest effect on the result.

The balanced scorecard shows in graphical form the relationships between the different factors being measured, which makes it all the more important to understand the impact and implications of one action on another. A good metric hierarchy and a thorough understanding of the context of the metrics allows the interactions to be properly interpreted.

Collaboration tools

New collaboration software tools, such as Microsoft Teams, Microsoft OneDrive, SharePoint, Yammer and Slack, can be valuable in communicating and sharing metrics across the organisation. Intranets are also valuable: their restricted access makes them a particularly useful channel for internal communications because they allow instantaneous transfer of electronically-held information, while extranets extend this capacity to suppliers and distributors too.

ACTIVITY 12

Do some research to find examples of organisations that actively discuss how they use the balanced scorecard. Do you think they discuss the factors they include in sufficient detail to allow them to assess whether they really are core contributors to the business objectives? Also consider whether they are using the balanced scorecard in the form intended by Kaplan and Norton, or if they have modified it to better fit their context and requirements.

4.3

MARKETING DASHBOARDS

Marketing dashboards, which we referred to in section 2.2, are graphical descriptions of data and information demonstrating performance and trends, which managers can use to inform strategic and operational decision-making. They have become more popular partly as a result of the ready availability of dashboards of online marketing information.

The essence of a dashboard is to capture key performance indicators in a visually intuitive and easily-understandable way. Rich in graphs and tables, a dashboard can contain a range of information, both financial and non-financial, that a variety of people can use to measure, monitor and manage activity. Because a dashboard demonstrates the progress an organisation is making towards achieving objectives, it should be updated as and when required.

You can create a dashboard in a variety of different ways, using either specific software (which may be free or paid for) or the charting software that comes as part of many business application programme packages. A dashboard should contain the vital information needed to present the current situation and to inform progress at three levels:

- Strategic – Measuring progress towards business and marketing objectives.
- Operational – Tracking the delivery of objectives and strategy in the operational marketing plan.
- Tactical – Monitoring delivery of the marketing tactics and projects that deliver the strategy.

A dashboard may be created for an organisation as a whole or for individual departments, so its design should therefore be tailored around the specific metrics or KPIs being used for decision-making in a given area. Because a dashboard presents complex data and metrics visually, it's crucial to plan and research a good design that, above all, allows key information to be clearly communicated to users and makes supporting information easily accessible.

Pre- and post-deployment dashboard testing
Dashboards need to be tested to ensure they are reporting:

- Correctly – The information obtained and reported matches the reality of the situation.
- Appropriately – The data reported is needed by and provides information to those who require it.

You therefore need to benchmark the data obtained and test the dashboard before using it fully. Steps suggested by Hemann and Burbary (2013) for conducting good benchmark research are:

- Set a goal – Ensure the goal is measurable and meets a strategic or operational requirement.
- Pick the tools – Establish the most appropriate tools for collecting and analysing the data.
- Conduct the research – Collect and analyse the data.
- Develop key findings – Filter the data to provide actionable insight that will allow you to start developing strategies.
- Establish additional research needs – Develop additional questions or hypotheses that require further testing and address these questions.

Dashboards and their applications

Dashboards can be used to display metrics results for a variety of areas, including the following:

- **Financial dashboards** – Are used to demonstrate current financial factors and trends, and include time periods appropriate for short-term monitoring – daily, monthly or quarterly figures, for example. Typical measures include **revenue**, **gross profit** and **return on sales**. Net profit is not easy to measure on a dashboard, as the tax and interest position is not calculated over the short time periods normally represented in a dashboard.
- **Brand and market dashboards** – Used to demonstrate brand sentiment and market performance, these help to monitor the current strength of the brand by considering trends in customer and market behaviour and current customer attitudes to the brand, based on measures such as **market share**, **market growth** and the **Net Promoter Score**®.
- **Product and pricing dashboards** – Show the sales and penetration of particular products, linking closely to price and promotional activity in order to demonstrate the effect changes in one area have on other areas. These dashboards also provide an understanding of the trend in the balance of products being sold, enabling marketers to monitor shifts in consumer purchases and to understand metrics such as **usage** and the **cannibalisation rate**.
- **Sales funnel dashboards** – A standard part of web analytics, these can cover all the metrics associated with the sales funnel to enable the marketer to quickly view the current pipeline and calculate the future potential business based on the number of customers at each stage of the funnel.
- **Channel dashboards** – Are used to demonstrate the current state of sales through channels and, where appropriate, specific intermediaries used by the organisation. They can cover, for example, the average sales value, volume, inventory and order levels to give a snapshot of channel activity.

- **Media dashboards** – Demonstrate the effectiveness (in terms of customer engagement and interaction) of media channels, in particular social media and online activity, along with advertising spend and rates of return (in terms of cost per click and cost per order).

Benefits of using dashboards include:

- Simple, intuitive and visual presentation of KPIs that can be easily interpreted.
- Allow managers to identify, highlight and correct negative trends.
- Through the use of tools such as 'drill down', allow more detailed reports to be generated.
- Facilitate more informed decision-making.
- Less time-consuming than running multiple reports.

The look, feel and content of a dashboard will typically evolve over time depending on the availability of data and the organisation's strategy and key measures/metrics. If your organisation or department is not currently reporting KPIs, start on a small scale and build upwards. Present only relevant data that people can use to make effective decisions. Include comparisons or targets – this year's performance versus last year's, for example, or performance against budget, to give the data a meaningful context.

Integrating multiple metrics into holistic dashboards

The main benefit of a dashboard is that it allows you to integrate multiple metrics in a single place, providing a holistic view of any given situation.

For a very good example of a dashboard (this one monitors the health of an email list), click on the following link: http://www.experian.com/blogs/marketing-forward/2013/03/15/want-to-increase-your-email-frequency-know-your-list-health/

When employees can see the results of the strategies and goals they have been working towards represented clearly and simply on a dashboard, it helps to build their engagement because it makes explicit the link between their contribution and the overall strategy. Also, clear dashboard results can give an organisation a significant competitive advantage, because managers have information at their fingertips on which to act quickly.

The balanced scorecard is a great example of integration, linking as it does the four elements of finance, customers, internal and innovation in a way that enables the effect of one to be seen on the others. This principle should be applied to all areas within dashboards. An example of a simple balanced scorecard dashboard is shown in Fig 4.2.

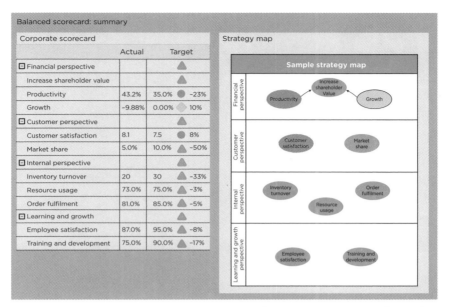

Balanced scorecard: summary

Corporate scorecard	Actual	Target	
⊟ Financial perspective		🔺	
Increase shareholder value		🔺	
Productivity	43.2%	35.0% ●	–23%
Growth	–9.88%	0.00% ◆	10%
⊟ Customer perspective		🔺	
Customer satisfaction	8.1	7.5 ●	8%
Market share	5.0%	10.0% 🔺	–50%
⊟ Internal perspective		🔺	
Inventory turnover	20	30 🔺	–33%
Resource usage	73.0%	75.0% 🔺	–3%
Order fulfilment	81.0%	85.0% 🔺	–5%
⊟ Learning and growth		🔺	
Employee satisfaction	87.0%	95.0% 🔺	–8%
Training and development	75.0%	90.0% 🔺	–17%

Fig 4.2 A balanced scorecard dashboard (*http://technet.microsoft.com/en-us/library/hh750382(v=office.14).aspx [accessed August 2014]*)

Reliance on dashboards

Because a dashboard provides only the main information from metrics it is not a complete picture; it is a selection of highlights chosen as being the most significant and relevant information for the intended audience. You can compare a marketing metrics dashboard to the dashboard on a car (that's where the name comes from, after all). The car dashboard indicates current 'key performance indicators' to the driver, but at times the driver needs to have the car plugged into a diagnostics computer to obtain a fuller set of readings, which may indicate developing areas of concern. Similarly, to really understand a marketing dashboard you sometimes have to go behind the main 'display' and do a more general audit of performance measures right across the organisation to ensure that developments in its macro and micro environments haven't increased the significance of other metrics to the extent that they need to be regularly included on the main dashboard too.

ACTIVITY 13

Based on the metrics you identified in Activity 6 (Chapter 1) what would you include in a dashboard to demonstrate the current situation and trends in an area for which information is available? What format would you use to present each piece of information to enable the status to be quickly and easily recognised?

Based on a current dashboard used in your organisation what areas could be important to investigate to ensure the most relevant information is displayed, and what triggers could require further investigation? If you don't use dashboards, how does your organisation communicate triggers for areas of concern, and how could the system be improved?

QUICK QUIZ – CHECK YOUR KNOWLEDGE

Questions
1. How does data integration benefit customer insight?
2. How fast is the volume of business data growing, according to IDC?
3. What four dimensions does the balanced scorecard measure?
4. What is a dashboard in marketing metrics terms?
5. What should it be possible to calculate based on a sales funnel dashboard?
6. What sources of information are used in the start-up stage of an organisation?
7. How much of Amazon's sales revenues accrued directly from cross-selling and upselling initiatives in 2006?

Answers
1. Higher conversion rates, improved retention rates and an overall ability to improve customer service.
2. The volume of business data worldwide doubles in size every two years, and by 2020 the digital universe will reach 44 zettabytes, or 44 trillion gigabytes.
3. Innovation and learning, internal perspective, customer perspective, financial perspective.
4. A graphical display used to collate the results of marketing metrics and present useful information for the organisation.
5. The future potential business based on the number of customers at each stage of the funnel.
6. Awareness, factors influencing customer advocacy, responses to promotional offers, how the product or service is used.
7. 35%.

BIBLIOGRAPHY

Anon (ND) *Balanced scorecard basics*. Balanced Scorecard Institute.
http://balancedscorecard.org/Resources/About-the-Balanced-Scorecard

Anon (2011) Created a balanced scorecard using dashboard designer. Microsoft
http://technet.microsoft.com/en-us/library/hh750382(v=office.14)

C&M Consulting Group (2014) 3 metrics your startup should be tracking. http://cmglobalgrp.com/1/post/2014/04/-3-metrics-your-startup-should-be-tracking.html [Accessed 2014]

IDC (2014) The digital universe opportunities: rich data and the increasing value of the Internet of Things. April.
https://www.emc.com/leadership/digital-universe/2014iview/executive-summary.htm

Kaplan, R.S. and Norton, D.P. (1992) The balanced scorecard – measures that drive performance. *Harvard Business Review*, Jan/Feb, Vol70(1), pp71-79.

Hemann, C. and Burbary, K. (2013) *Digital marketing analytics: making sense of consumer data in a digital world.* QUE.

Nguyen, C. (2013) Want to increase your email frequency? Know your list health!
http://www.experian.com/blogs/marketing-forward/2013/03/15/want-to-increase-your-email-frequency-know-your-list-health/

5.0
USING METRICS TO MEASURE EFFECTIVENESS AND INFORM DECISION-MAKING

This chapter explains how to apply marketing metrics to establish the effectiveness of marketing activities. At the end of this chapter you will be able to:

- Understand the importance of measurement and accountability.
- Understand how to apply different types of marketing metrics to inform tactical activity.
- Plan and analyse marketing activities.
- Modify marketing activities.
- Understand automated techniques for reacting to metrics.

117

MEASUREMENT AND ACCOUNTABILITY

CEOs, CFOs and others are increasingly demanding greater accountability from marketers – and if marketers can't produce the goods they shouldn't be surprised if their budgets are cut. This is bad news for everyone, of course: marketing is about identifying and satisfying customer needs, at a profit, and profitable products and services create sustainably healthy organisations.

Numbers are the language of business, so it makes sense that marketers adopt a more quantitative approach to the development of marketing plans and associated activities than may have traditionally been the case. They need to be able to explain, justify and, where appropriate, support with numbers, their plans and progress – what's been done, being done, will be done; why, how, when and by whom; and with what results.

There is an inexorable logic to the process.

1. Quantifying and measuring the value of marketing programmes and investments
2. Improves the efficiency and effectiveness of marketing
3. Grows customer knowledge, insight and conversion
4. Improves the allocation and ROI of marketing spend
5. Allow the organisation to extract greater value and profitability from customer relationships
6. All of which increases the credibility, influence and perceived value of marketing and its practitioners in the eyes of senior management – which, in turn, leads to a greater willingness to invest further in marketing. It's a virtuous circle.

The good news is that technological advances have made it possible for marketers to measure everything they need to measure, even in real time, and this allows them to create marketing strategies and tactics that are financially justifiable in the C-suite.

The American Marketing Association defines marketing accountability as: "the responsibility for the systematic management of marketing resources and processes to achieve measurable gains in return on marketing investment and increased marketing efficiency, while maintaining quality and increasing the value of the corporation."

APPLYING MARKETING METRICS TO INFORM TACTICAL ACTIVITY

McDonald and Mouncey (2009) define a marketing metrics model that has five key areas:

- Corporate performance.
- Market segments.
- Impact factors.
- Marketing and other actions.
- Budget resource.

This is illustrated in Fig 5.1:

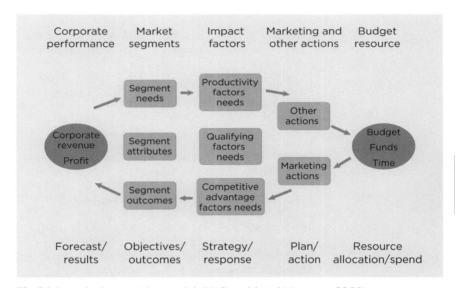

Fig 5.1 A marketing metrics model *(McDonald and Mouncey, 2009)*

The elements of the model work together as follows:

- **Corporate performance** captures the goals and associated metrics at corporate level that relate to marketing activities.
- **Market segments** help to identify target groups, so that appropriate objectives can be set and resources deployed in the areas where most value is added for the customer and organisation.
- **Impact factors** include:
  - Qualifying factors, which are the prerequisites (from a customer perspective) for being included in the sector.
  - Competitive advantage factors, which focus on customer needs and really matter to customers.
  - Productivity factors, which are essentially about reducing costs.

- **Marketing and other actions** enhance the impact factors to facilitate the achievement of the strategy.
- **Resource** is required to deliver the actions.

These stages comprise an iterative process.

Defining the feedback loop – Feedback is provided in the model above through a measurement strategy based on the metrics discussed elsewhere in this study guide. The feedback loop enables marketers to monitor a change in one element against overall results to determine whether or not the change made a difference, and helps them to understand whether the same activity should be repeated or needs to be modified in order to create greater success.

Feedback loops use results to improve things for the future. This brings us back to the true purpose of metrics, which is to help us understand what has happened and to use that information to inform future plans and strategies.

Creating a test and learn environment – According to the McDonald and Mouncey (2009) model, marketers need to develop metrics for each major stage:

- **Corporate performance and segments** – You need to verify and research the segments and then develop metrics that are relevant to the characteristics of the segment, to the market position of the organisation and to the opportunities and threats facing it. You need to test these before moving on to the next stage.
- **Impact factors** – You need to determine specific metrics for the impact factors and establish the links between the factors. Again, you should test these before moving on to the next stage.
- **Actions and resources** – You need to ensure that all marketing actions are based on meeting the objectives for the impact factors, and develop fully-costed progress metrics for all actions. You should test the links between the impact factors and actions.

You can then create a finalised set of metrics that have passed all the tests.

However, this is a continuous learning process whereby the results of one review of corporate performance are used to create inputs for the future. To help this continuous improvement process, it is useful to apply a concept such as the Plan, Do, Check, Act (PDCA) cycle popularised by Deming, or Kolb's learning cycle. These cycles are iterative, so the outcome of every cycle informs the next one on a continuous basis, with measurement and results improving with each iteration.

When applied to the development of metrics the PDCA cycle allows managers to analyse activity in order to identify the causes of errors, and if it is adopted as an iterative approach it then allows feedback to be used to ascertain both the success of changes made and the utility of the metrics used.

Assessing effectiveness – An overriding purpose of metrics is to assess effectiveness. Data can be generated to reflect the contributions made by individual products, brands, territories, channels, sales representatives, market segments and so on. To measure the effectiveness of particular marketing actions, data is needed to identify which outcomes and, where applicable, profits, have occurred as a result.

The ultimate measure of the effectiveness of marketing, in a commercial organisation, is some sort of financial return – typically increased sales and profitability.

5.3

PLAN, ANALYSE AND MODIFY MARKETING ACTIVITIES BASED ON METRICS ANALYSIS

The behaviour of customers, suppliers and other stakeholders is not consistent; it changes over time. When planning marketing activities you need to monitor trends affecting all stakeholders in order to be able to react to those that are significant.

Within the rapidly evolving digital marketing sphere, for example, you need to monitor how people search and what they search for because such patterns reflect changing trends, and you can make continuous small changes to online materials accordingly. As we discussed earlier, there is a wealth of search tools available to help you understand trends in online behaviour, and search data on your own organisations and those of competitors is readily available.

Tracking trends

Among the range of free tools available for tracking online trends are the following:

- Google Trends – Identifies popular search trends based on Google search queries. Go to www.google.com/trends and enter the search term 'marketing metrics' to see examples. Alternatively, try this: http://www.google.com/trends/explore#q=marketing%20metrics
- YouTube Trends – Described by YouTube as "a new destination for the latest trending videos and video trends ... and a resource for daily insight into what is happening with web video." Look at www.youtube.com/trendsdashboard for examples.
- Google AdWords Keyword Tool – Integrated into the Google AdWords platform the Keyword Tool is useful to inform and refine advertising through Google, but also helps marketers explore the brand associations made. Look at www.google.co.uk/adwords or click on the following link for a typical Google Adwords Keyword Tool report: http://adwords.blogspot.fr/2013/05/introducing-keyword-planner-combining.html

Many organisations learn by watching for trending data on their own key performance indicators (KPIs). Starting small, you can use Google Analytics on a couple of KPIs and look at the trends to spot any emerging patterns. Trends and patterns are good indicators of competitive strengths and weaknesses that can help to differentiate an organisation.

The key requirement when tracking trends is to use the information gained to make decisions and improve future plans. Trends can appear in any area monitored by metrics and are a reason why dashboards should not just reflect the current situation but also feature graphs to show historic data. Once you've spotted a trend you need to monitor and assess it to see if is statistically significant before you act on it – although more entrepreneurial marketers might choose to react to the early 'weak signals' of an emerging trend in order to gain 'first mover' advantage.

ACTIVITY 15

How many of these measurement methods are used within your own organisation, and if they aren't used why is that the case? Imagine you had to construct an argument for including these measurements within the metrics your organisation uses: what would be the advantages and disadvantages of each method in relation to your own organisation's activities?

Modelling and forecasting

Analysing data from metrics enables an organisation to understand its current situation. However, in order to plan effectively it has to develop a view of the future, which is where forecasting comes in. Forecasts can be based on metrics, but they can also inform the metrics required. While they are unlikely to be important in the day-to-day operations of the organisation, forecasts are vital to determine long-term direction.

Forecasting is the process of using available information to project (or predict) a view of the future. It uses a number of techniques, either independently or in combination, depending on the situation to be forecast. Forecasting provides quantified estimates that can form the base for marketing objectives and plans.

Essentially there are two views of the future:

- It will follow the same trends as it did in the past.
- It will be radically different from the past.

Forecasting has to take into account both possibilities, and provide techniques to support them both.

Forecasting can be either quantitative or qualitative:

- Quantitative forecasting – Relies on numbers, or 'raw data', and attempts to extrapolate from these future trends and the probability of events happening.
- Qualitative forecasting – Is used where there is no data available, and relies mainly on human judgement and expert opinions to provide a likely view of the future.

Forecasting is different from research. Research helps you to understand the past and the present in order to assess what customers might think and do in the future. But for longer-term, more strategic issues, where customer information is less readily available and less reliable, the value of research is limited (although research can provide the data on which to base forecasts). This is where forecasting helps.

Forecasting techniques include:

- **Trend extrapolation** – Also known as **time series analysis**, this is a statistical technique that examines past trends in the market and extrapolates them into the future. Trend extrapolation can be used to identify:
  - Seasonal and other cyclical fluctuations.
  - Long-term underlying trends.
- **Modelling** – This is an analytical approach that uses historic information, such as point-of-sale data and companies' internal data, to quantify the sales impact of various marketing activities. This

generates a set of assumptions (for example, every £1 of advertising generates £2.36 of sales) which can then be input to a model of future plans to establish whether they are likely to be profitable. To make sure the assumptions used are robust, substantial statistical analysis is necessary – including complex 'multiple regression analysis' – but many online resources, including proprietary programmes, can be used to support the necessary work.

Testing and analysis

One of the most popular testing elements in marketing is **A/B testing** – a technique used for many years in advertising and direct marketing but now mainly associated with digital marketing. In simple terms A/B testing involves testing two alternatives to see which delivers the greater success against a desired metric. In digital marketing this can be web pages, but it could equally be variations of an offline advert, different wording in a direct communication etc. As an example, an organisation may have two different appeals in two different pieces of copy for a product. It sends the B alternative to 10% of the mailing list, and if this gives a better response than the A alternative (that everyone else received) by a statistically significant margin, then the copy in the B alternative is clearly the copy to use for the next mailing. However, the organisation can vary the copy in the next mailing too to see if it can do better again. For the sake of accuracy only one variable should be changed when using A/B testing.

A/B testing provides great insights into how strategies and tactics affect the organisation's results. However, as with all measures, you need good metrics and analysis to ensure you define the variables correctly for the requirements of the test, and you need to create specific variables for each test. You also need to use statistical significance (see explanation in Chapter 6) in A/B testing to ensure the results are viable. In addition, it is essential that the metric being determined by the testing is accurately defined and has a measurable element that clearly differentiates the two areas being compared.

A/B testing is often used for search engine optimisation or pay per click advertising – you would make a small change or have two variations to see which is the more effective. This can be extended to **multivariate testing**, which digital marketers use to ensure the offers, content and layout are optimised for visitors. Multivariate testing enables multiple combinations and variations of web-page elements to be tested simultaneously, rather than the single element that is tested in A/B testing. Multivariate testing allows marketers to select the most effective combination of page design elements to achieve the desired goal.

You have to analyse the results of A/B testing carefully, and consider whether any other variables may have been present that might have skewed the results. You have to be certain that the results were attributable to the elements you meant to test, and here human interpretation is essential.

ACTIVITY 16

Has your organisation conducted A/B testing on any elements of the website and, if so, what were the results? If not, which areas (or if it has, which *other* areas) would lend themselves to A/B testing, and what variations would you use? What would you measure to assess the result of the test?

Supporting changes in the planning and implementation stages

Ultimately you could argue that the purpose of metrics is to support changes in planning and strategy implementation. Your past results, as indicated through the metrics, form the basis for decisions about the future.

The four-stage planning model APIC (Analysis, Planning, Implementation, Control) can be used to demonstrate the use of metrics:

- **Analysis** – Collecting data and information and analysing it to understand the current situation. This data and information is provided by internal and external metrics:
  - Internal metrics will include, for example, financial information and the results of previous marketing activities, including metrics relating to the way the 7P marketing mix is used and the way the different elements interact with each other.
  - External metrics will be derived from measuring and benchmarking competitors, and from analysis of macro-environmental factors such as economic, social and demographic change.
- **Planning** – Using the information from metrics to develop objectives, strategies and tactics (covering the extended 7P marketing mix) for the plan period. The strategy should be:
  - Derived from the metrics and benchmark research.
  - Measurable, based on SMART objectives.
  - Easily broken down into tactical components, which can be integrated.
  - Integrated, with all the components having synergy with each other.
  - Measurable – the tactical elements should all have clear metrics so that success can be measured.

- **Implementation** – Putting the plan in place and taking actions to deliver the tactics, including generating metrics to demonstrate success.
- **Control** – Using the metrics to determine the next steps and where amendments are needed to ensure the objectives (provided they are still relevant) are delivered.

5.4

PLAN AND ANALYSE AUTOMATED TECHNIQUES FOR REACTING TO METRICS

Van Rijn and Chaffey (2014) define marketing automation as follows:

"Marketing automation enables businesses to automate customer communications activities as part of the marketing and sales process. The use of marketing automation services makes new, more sophisticated processes and relevant communication and experiences possible across a range of touchpoints across the customer lifecycle. More relevant contextual experiences and offers promise an increase in return-on-investment from customer communications and increased efficiency in marketing teams with time savings from manual campaign activities."

Many areas of marketing can be automated:

- Email:
  - Email personalisation.
  - Real-time triggered emails based on actions taken by customers or prospects.
  - Dynamic content and response measurement.
- Database:
  - More than just a CRM system, a database should include all the contact and communication details about customers and prospects.
  - Website visits and email clicks should be recorded in the database.
- Lead capture, management and nurturing:
  - Integrated with offline activity.
- Automated sales alerts and tasks.
- Programme management:
  - Manage multiple channel marketing campaigns and programmes including online advertising, video, mobile and social media.

In many contexts marketing automation is used to refer to software platforms and technologies that automate marketing processes, but although this is a major element of automation, automation involves much more than this. Setting up and maintaining automation takes time and effort, because you need to use the metrics generated to continually improve the automation, incorporating areas such as A/B testing for all the interactions, and integrating activities and measures.

The growth in digital marketing has been accompanied by a rise in the amount of marketing data and information that can be automated. But however much automation you have, you need to manage it to ensure you're getting the right results. Crucially, you need to maintain a customer-centric approach, otherwise the benefits of automation will be wasted. What's more, not everything can be automated, and marketers should keep front of mind the need to deliver business goals through satisfying customer requirements.

So adopting automation therefore becomes a change management activity. There are many models of change but one of the most relevant ones to integrating metrics and automation, despite its age, is the four-phase model of planned change from Bullock and Battern (1958), cited in Burnes (1996).

The model explains change in terms of two dimensions:

- Change phases – the stages through which an organisation moves in any planned change.
- Change processes – the means by which an organisation moves from one state to the next.

Let's look at the change phases and processes below, in relation to marketing automation.

1. **Exploration phase** – The stage during which the organisation will decide whether to automate more of its marketing activities, and, if it does, allocate resources to the process. *The change processes* during this phase may include becoming aware of the need to adopt automation and searching for external help.
2. **Planning phase** – Understanding why the organisation needs to automate its marketing activities. *The change processes* involved here may include searching for information to fully understand the situation, establishing objectives and gaining the support of key decision-makers.
3. **Action phase** – The changes required for marketing automation are implemented. Arrangements are established to manage the change process, gain staff support, evaluate the implementation and take corrective action if necessary.
4. **Integration phase** – Developing a new status quo. *The change processes* for marketing automation are reinforced by communication and encouraging improvements and new behaviour through reward systems.

Automating marketing processes and integrating them with metrics is not the work of a moment. It takes time, planning and the involvement of a range of different people to embed the required new ways of working. McDonald and Mouncey (2009) suggest the following key team members for implementing the marketing measurement model:

- Market research manager.
- Corporate planning manager.
- Corporate finance manager.
- Customer database manager.
- Market planning manager.
- Finance manager (with responsibility for marketing).
- Marketing communications/advertising manager.
- Senior marketing manager.

- Customer service or operations manager.
- Brand, product or customer segment manager.

In a smaller organisation one person will carry out several of these roles. One notable absence from the list is a representative from the IT department. While this is understandable in that the inputs are primarily commercial, including someone from IT might yield valuable input and buy-in.

The link between marketing and sales needs particularly close management during the marketing automation process. A marketing automation system will capture lead information that the sales team can use to close sales, so it's essential to ensure that there is integration and buy-in between the parties involved. The sales team need to trust and act on the information from the system, as well as feed information back into it based on interactions with customers and prospects.

Examples of automated techniques that help interpret marketing metrics include scenario planning, attribution modelling and dashboards.

Scenario planning and planned reactions

Scenario planning is a technique for trying to prepare the organisation for the future by understanding the nature and impact of some of the most uncertain yet important forces likely to affect it. It is concerned with identifying a number of possible futures, rather than adopting a single view. It is a group process that encourages the exchange of knowledge and the development of deeper understanding of issues that are central to the future of the business.

The 'what if' modelling it involves allows the team to produce different scenarios, from the safe to the more imaginative, with contingency plans for addressing them. Scenario planning serves the twin purpose of increasing managers' knowledge of the business environment and widening their awareness about possible future events. It is typically used by organisations that have to make expensive long-term decisions in uncertain situations.

Broad scenario planning steps:

1. Identify the drivers for change based on metrics used within the organisation and external sources of information.
2. Bring the drivers together into a viable framework that links various outcomes.
3. Produce seven to nine mini scenarios to demonstrate the future possibilities.
4. Group mini-scenarios into two or three larger scenarios through determining similarities within the scenarios.
5. Fully explore each of the scenarios.
6. Identify issues arising.

ACTIVITY 17

Think about an everyday task within your own role, and attempt a scenario planning exercise on it. How many possible scenarios could arise, and is your organisation currently planning for these?

Attribution modelling

'Marketing attribution' is used to quantify the influence each element of marketing communication, both on- and offline, has on a customer's decision to buy something or convert from one product or service option to another. Attribution is a process that identifies actions (or events) by current or potential customers that contribute towards the purchase or conversion decision, with a value assigned to each of the events.

Attribution modelling allows marketers to optimise the use of those resources that return the highest conversion, and at the same time to compare different elements and channels. Understanding the customer journey across the whole marketing mix, and in particular the promotional elements, allows marketers to gain a more accurate picture than they would from analysing data from each mix element individually. The attribution data can be used to plan future campaigns, providing a balance between all activities, online and offline, to ensure the right customer touchpoints are in place, using the most cost-effective ones as demonstrated through metrics such as **cost per action**.

An example of a digital journey is illustrated in Fig 5.2.

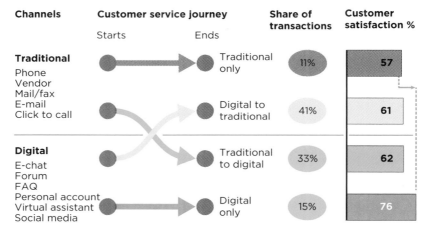

Fig 5.2 An example of a digital journey (*Bianchi, 2014*)

5.5

Real-time data analysis

Real-time analysis is a relatively new capability within digital marketing, and it does what the name suggests – analyses data in real time, with a specific focus on what users are doing on a website now.

Google offers real-time analytics via its Google Analytics pages, which many organisations use to understand their website visitors. In Google's own words: "The reports are updated continuously and each page view is reported seconds after it occurs on your site. For example, you can see:

- How many people are on your site right now.
- Their geographic locations and the traffic sources that referred them.
- Which pages or events they're interacting with.
- Which goal conversions have occurred.

With real-time, you can immediately and continuously monitor the effects that new campaigns and site changes have on your traffic. Here are a few of the ways that you might use real-time:

- Monitor whether new and changed content on your site is being viewed.
- Understand usage of your mobile app through event tracking.
- See whether a one-day promotion is driving traffic to your site or app, and which pages these visitors are viewing.
- Monitor the immediate effects on traffic from a blog/social network post or tweet.
- Verify that the tracking code is working on your site or app.
- Monitor goal completions as you test changes to your site."

With real-time analytics you can quickly observe, analyse and optimise a website through seeing what is happening now rather than waiting for the traditional analytics reporting delays.

However, there are both advantages and disadvantages to real-time data.

Advantages include:

- You can spot issues and errors very quickly – if a web-link is broken, for example, it will show through the real-time data and can be corrected quickly.
- Where real-time data includes observing the competition, you'll get instant notification of changes in strategy and price.
- When monitoring online traffic in real time, you can implement changes immediately to increase conversion rates and revenue. Similarly, you can respond immediately to comments and questions.

- You can save costs, because, provided the system has been implemented correctly, the information you need is instantly available, meaning you don't need to wait for information or spend time actioning requests.
- Better insights into current sales and conversion levels allow you to take actions to prevent missing out on sales because of low stock levels, for example, or losing revenue by selling too much at too low a price when stock is scarce.
- You can understand customer trends more fully and act on them using decisions informed by analytics that reflect the current trend.

However, these advantages are countered to some extent by the disadvantages of using real-time data. You need to weigh the advantages against the disadvantages before and while you use real-time data.

- Full real-time analysis may require significant computing power. Google Real-Time analytics may not require extra capability, but full implementation of real-time analytics across an organisation can demand large processing capability.
- Real-time insights require a different culture and ways of working. You need to act quickly to take advantage of the benefits of real-time information but this may not come naturally to people who are used to getting information on a weekly or monthly basis. You may need to take much shorter-term decisions than you would without real-time data, which means that your conventional decision-making processes may no longer be appropriate.
- A change spotted in real time may not be significant – it could be a one-off event that doesn't need responding to. If you do act on it, it may give you the wrong outcome.

Security is a potential issue as much real-time data is provided through the Cloud. You must protect information stored in or accessed by the Cloud environment as it may be available to those outside the organisation if policies and procedures are not carefully thought through and applied. An organisation may be liable for any breaches of customer data privacy, which can also cause significant negative publicity.

Tracking social media sentiment to adjust pricing, availability and brand positioning

Sentiment analysis is the evaluation of content posted on social media to determine whether the views – 'sentiment' – of the poster are positive or negative. The purpose is to understand subjective opinions about an organisation, brand, product, topic and so on, so as to adjust things, where necessary, to improve those perceptions.

Software can carry out sentiment analysis, but this may be only 70% accurate primarily because of the way language is used and interpreted. For example, a post such as "I really enjoyed the meal at the restaurant this evening; the food was fantastic," can fairly easily be interpreted as positive, given the two unambiguously positive statements it contains. If the post was longer, however, and included two negative points – say, "The service was disappointing and the bill was extortionate," then the sentiment becomes harder to rate overall. Do two positives and two negatives make this a neutral post? Overall what it probably shows is that the restaurant is doing very well with food and the eating experience, but needs to look at the service it provides and consider whether its pricing is correct.

The way language is used can also make it difficult to interpret sentiment, particularly when commentators are sarcastic, as many of them are in social media. "I always love it when the waiter brings the wrong food" has a positive element – "I always love it" – but as expressed here it is clearly negative. Human beings can pick up such nuances, but software can find them very difficult to interpret.

Social 'listening' tools can help in understanding sentiment, but human beings are likely to deliver a more accurate result.

ACTIVITY 18
Look at recent posts on social media about your organisation or one that you're familiar with and determine the sentiment in relation to aspects of the brand, to give an overall rating. Identify another organisation that you feel does this well, and consider what they do that your organisation could learn from, and how you might adapt their methods to suit your own organisational context.

Technology and platform integration
There are already software platforms that integrate applications and services – many tools for social media integrate into one-screen feeds for multiple Twitter, Facebook, LinkedIn and other social media content and metrics, for example. One example is Hootsuite, which provides analytics in many different forms for a range of social media platforms. An area that has been talked about but has yet to be developed into a commercial proposition is a tool that integrates full social media listening capability with the ability to engage in real time and to collect data on the interactions.

Traditional and digital metric integration
We've discussed online and offline metrics throughout this textbook, but ideally they should not be seen as separate areas but integrated into one set of analysis. According to Vaughan (2012), Mike Volpe of Hubspot states:

"Web analytics measure things a webmaster cares about, like page load times, page views per visit, and time on site. Marketing analytics, on the other hand, measure business metrics like traffic, leads and sales, and which events (both on and off your website) influence whether leads become customers. Marketing analytics include data not only from your website, but also from other sources like email, social media, and even offline events. Marketing analytics are also usually people-centric, featuring the prospect, lead or customer as the unit of focus, whereas web analytics usually regard the page view as the unit of focus in its reports."

This implies that it is marketing analytics, not web analytics, that we should be thinking about – because integrated online and offline metrics provide a wider view on which to make marketing decisions. This is certainly a trend in holistic analytics, with services from Google and others providing integration of online and offline analytics.

Integrated analytics can recognise the contribution made by offline marketing activity, particularly promotion to direct customers to purchase online. They can also help the marketer to understand the online journey that leads a customer to pick up the phone to place an order or visit a store to buy something.

The key benefit of integrated metrics is the wider understanding they give, enabling better decision-making, which may well lead to further integration of activities and therefore be an additional driver for further integration of metrics.

ACTIVITY 19

Investigate the potential platforms and software available for integrating metrics and analyse the options to determine the most suitable one/s to use within your organisation.

QUICK QUIZ – CHECK YOUR KNOWLEDGE

Questions
1. What is the purpose of a feedback loop?
2. What is the ultimate criterion for measuring the effectiveness of marketing in a commercial organisation?
3. What free tools can be used for tracking online trends?
4. How does forecasting differ from research?
5. Define A/B testing.
6. What does APIC stand for?
7. What does Google Analytics allow a user to see in real time?
8. What does sentiment assist with the understanding of?

Answers

1. Allows a change in one element of a process to be monitored against overall results to determine whether or not the change makes a difference, and, if so, what, to inform decision-making.
2. A commercial return, in the form of increased sales and profitability.
3. Google Trends, YouTube Trends, Google AdWords Keyword Tool.
4. Research is about understanding past and present events to gather information about customer perceptions of the future, whereas forecasting predicts the future.
5. The testing of two alternatives to see which one returns the greater success against a desired metric.
6. Analysis, Planning, Implementation, Control.
7. How many people are on your site right now, their geographic locations and the traffic sources that referred them, the pages or events they're interacting with, and the goal conversions that have occurred.
8. Subjective opinions relating to how people feel about an organisation, brand, product, topic or similar.

BIBLIOGRAPHY

Bianchi, R., Schiavotto, D., Svoboda, D. (2014) Why companies should care about e-care. *McKinsey & Company,* August. http://www.mckinsey.com/business-functions/marketing-and-sales/our-insights/why-companies-should-care-about-ecare

Burnes, B. (1996) *Managing change.* London, Financial Times Management.

Deming, W.E. (1993) *The new economics for industry, government and education.* Boston, MIT Press. p132

Kolb, D.A., Rubin, I.M. and McIntyre, J.M. (1974) *Organizational psychology: a book of readings.* 2nd edition. Englewood Cliffs, Prentice-Hall.

McDonald, M and Mouncey, P. (2009) *Marketing accountability: a new metrics model to measure marketing effectiveness.* London, Kogan Page.

Van Rijn, J. and Chaffey, D. (2014) A definition of marketing automation in 2014, Smart Insights. http://www.smartinsights.com/lead-generation/marketing-automation/definition-marketing-automation/

Vaughan, P. (2012) Why you need marketing analytics not web analytics, Hubspot. http://blog.hubspot.com/blog/tabid/6307/bid/31705/Why-You-Need-Marketing-Analytics-Not-Web-Analytics.aspx

Google Trends
https://trends.google.com/trends/

Google Adwords
https://adwords.google.com/intl/en_uk/home/

YouTube
https://www.youtube.com/feed/trending

GLOSSARY OF TERMS

Average items per transaction – The number of items purchased per transaction.

$$\text{Average items per transaction} = \frac{\text{total number of items sold}}{\text{total number of transactions}}$$

Average sales value – The amount of money spent on average by website visitors.

$$\text{Average sales value} = \frac{\text{total revenue received via website}}{\text{number of website visitors}}$$

Average transaction size – Average financial value of each transaction made, expressed in currency terms.

$$\text{Average transaction size} = \frac{\text{total value of sales in time}}{\text{total number of transactions in time}}$$

Bounce rate – The number of people who leave a website after visiting the entry page.

Brand equity – Used to measure the value of a brand. There are many different ways to value a brand, so it is advisable to conduct research into the most appropriate method for the context.

Brand or price premium – The amount that can be charged for a branded product above the level for an unbranded one.

$$\text{Brand premium} = \frac{\text{average price of the branded product}}{\text{overall average price in the category}}$$

Cannibalisation rates – The reduction in sales of existing products when new products are introduced, either volume or value.

$$\text{Cannibalisation rate (\%)} = \frac{\text{sales lost from existing products}}{\text{sales of new product}}$$

Cash burn rate – Measures the amount of cash available until it runs out.

Churn – The percentage of customers or subscribers to a service that discontinue their subscription to that service in a given time period.

$$\text{Churn} = \frac{\text{the number of customers an organisation loses over time period}}{\text{the number of active customers at the start of the period}}$$

Compound annual growth rate (CAGR) – The growth in sales over time of an organisation

$$CAGR = \left(\frac{\text{final sales value}}{\text{starting sales value}} \right)\left(\frac{1}{\text{no. of years}} \right) - 1$$

Conversion rate – Measures the number of people who respond and then make a purchase.

$$\text{Conversion rate} = \frac{\text{number of people who respond and purchase}}{\text{number of people who respond to the message}}$$

Cost per click – The amount paid in pay-per-click advertising for each person following the link from the advert to the destination.

Cost per lead – The amount of money paid in advertising to gain a single lead.

$$\text{Cost per lead} = \frac{\text{total promotional spend}}{\text{number of leads generated}}$$

Customer acquisition/growth rate – Measures the conversion of enquiries to paying customers.

Customer lifetime value (CLV) – Total revenue from a customer over the duration of the organisation's entire relationship with that customer over a period of time.

$$CLV = \frac{\text{constant net margin}}{(\text{discount rate} + \text{constant defection rate})}$$

Customer satisfaction

Customer satisfaction – the number or percentage of customers reporting experience that exceeds specified satisfaction levels. Generally conducted through research.

Willingness to recommend – the percentage of surveyed customers who indicate they would be willing to recommend the brand to others.

Retention rate – the percentage of customers an organisation is able to retain over a specific time period.

$$\text{Retention rate} = \frac{\text{number of active customers at end of time period}}{\text{number of active customers at start of time period}}$$

Discount rate – The interest rate used in discounted cash flow (DCF) analysis to determine the present value of future cash flows.

Downloads – Numbers of people downloading an item from a web page.

Earnings per share (EPS) – The portion of a company's profit which is allocated to each outstanding share of common stock. This measure serves as an indicator of the company's profitability.

$$\text{Earnings per share} = \frac{\text{profit available to equity shareholders}}{\text{average number of issued equity shares}}$$

Funnel value – Potential value of prospective customers in the sales funnel.

Intermediary margin percentage – Measure of the profit margin intermediaries achieve, comparing their purchase with selling price.

$$\text{Intermediary margin (\%)} = \frac{\text{selling price to customer}}{\text{purchase price from supplier}}$$

Internal rate of return – The discount rate often used in capital budgeting that makes the net present value of all cash flows from a particular project equal to zero.

Inventory turnover and days *Inventory turnover* – measures how quickly inventory is sold, generally over the course of a year.

$$\text{Inventory turnover} = \frac{\text{sales}}{\text{average inventory}}$$

Inventory days – the number of day's worth of sales that the current inventory can supply.

$$\text{Inventory days} = \frac{\text{days in year (365)}}{\text{inventory turnover}}$$

Margin of error – The greatest predicted difference between an actual parameter and a sample estimate of that parameter. A margin of error is therefore usually accompanied by a statement of probability, often articulated in the form of a percentage confidence level.

Market demand – Total demand for a particular product or service.

$$\text{Market demand (during time period)} = \text{repeat or replacement purchases in period (£)} + \text{new purchases in period (£)}$$

Market growth – Total sales in market compared with previous periods.

$$\text{Growth (\%)} = \frac{\text{increase this year (volume or value)}}{\text{volume or value last year}}$$

Market penetration – Comparison of current versus potential market demand for products.

$$\text{Market penetration} = \frac{\text{current market demand}}{\text{potential market demand}}$$

Market share – *Market share* – sales of the organisation as a percentage of the total sales volume in the industry/sector/product/market.

$$\text{Market share} = \frac{\text{sales of organisation in time (volume or value)}}{\text{sum of all sales in time (volume or value)}}$$

Relative market share – performance of a brand versus key competitor.

$$\text{Relative market share} = \frac{\text{brand's market share (volume or value)}}{\text{largest competitor market share (volume or value)}}$$

Marketing cost per unit – Measures the amount of money spent on marketing in relation to the number of units of products or services sold.

$$\text{Marketing cost per unit} = \frac{\text{total marketing expense in time period}}{\text{total units sold in time period}}$$

Net present value – The difference between the present value of cash inflows and the present value of cash outflows. NPV is used in capital budgeting to analyse the profitability of an investment or project.

Net Promoter Score® (NPS®) – Is based on an assumption that an organisation's customers can be divided into three categories: promoters, passives and detractors. This classification is derived from one key advocacy question: 'How likely is it that you would recommend [the organisation] to a friend or colleague?' Customers respond on a 0 to 10-point rating scale and are classified as follows:

- Promoters (scoring 9-10 out of 10) are loyal enthusiasts who will keep buying and refer others to the organisation.
- Passives (scoring 7-8 out of 10) are satisfied but passive customers who are therefore potential switchers to competitors.
- Detractors (scoring 0-6 out of 10) are unhappy customers who can damage your brand through negative word-of-mouth.

New product adoption rate – Provides information about the rate of adoption of new products introduced by the organisation.

New product adoption rate = rate of penetration of potential x percentage of total market expected to buy product (1 – rate of penetration of potential) $^{\text{period of time} - 1}$

(Please see the core text for a worked example).

Page impressions – The number of times a page is viewed by people through the website; the total number of visitors to the website.

Price elasticity of demand – Measures the change in demand for a product in response to a change in price.

Pricing basket metrics – Pricing basket analysis is a technique for highlighting affinity relationships among products purchased together. The technique identifies associations between products or between categories that customers tend to purchase together 'complements', or between products that customers rarely purchase together 'substitutes'.

Product development response – The time taken to rectify any issues with products in response to customer feedback.

Profit impact – The impact on profits of product-related expenditure. It depends upon the manufacturing sales price and contribution.

Profit impact = (contribution per unit x units sold) – total fixed costs

Reach – The percentage of people in a target audience reached by a single exposure of a promotional message.

Recall – Measured through research, shows the number of people who recall seeing brand advertising *without* prompting.

Recognition – Measured through research, shows the number of people who recall seeing brand advertising *with* prompting.

Redemption rate – Measures the numbers of coupons redeemed in relation to the number issued.

$$\text{Redemption rate} = \frac{\text{number of coupons redeemed}}{\text{number of coupons issued}}$$

Response rate – Measures the number of people who respond to an offer related to those who received it.

$$\text{Response rate} = \frac{\text{number of people who respond to the message}}{\text{number of people exposed to the message}}$$

Return on capital employed (ROCE) – Measures profits before interest and tax in relation to the capital employed to generate that profit.

$$\text{ROCE} = \frac{\text{earnings before interest and tax (EBIT)}}{\text{capital employed}}$$

Return on investment (ROI) – Considers profit in relation to the investment required to generate that profit.

$$\text{ROI (\%)} = \frac{\text{net profit (£)}}{\text{investment (£)}}$$

Revenue and profit *Revenue* – the total income generated by an organisation from sales of products and services.

$$Revenue = $$
$$price\ of\ products\ or\ services \times quantity\ sold\ in\ time\ period$$

Gross profit – represents the total revenue less the costs of the goods incurred to generate the revenue.

$$Gross\ profit = revenue - cost\ of\ goods\ sold$$

Net profit – the final profit after all costs including taxes, selling costs, interest and any other costs incurred by the organisation are taken into account.

$$Net\ profit = revenue - total\ costs$$

Return on sales – measures the organisation's ability to generate profit from sales.

$$Return\ on\ sales = \frac{net\ profit\ before\ tax}{sales}$$

Sales per square foot/unit of floor area – Demonstrates the productivity of sales area in retail contexts.

$$Sales\ per\ square\ foot/metre = \frac{total\ sales}{selling\ area\ in\ square\ feet/metres}$$

Sales price variation – The variation in selling price from the recommended or target price.

$$Sales\ price\ variation = quantity\ sold\ (actual\ price\ during\ period - recommended\ price)$$

Share of voice – Compares the media spending by an organisation with the total expenditure for the product/service/category.

$$Share\ of\ voice = \frac{advertising\ spend\ by\ organisation\ over\ time\ period}{total\ of\ all\ advertising\ expenditure\ over\ time\ period}$$

Social media activity – Also known as social media engagement, this measures the numbers of engaged social media users.

$$Social\ media\ activity = \frac{active\ members}{total\ members}$$

Total clicks – The number of times a link included in a promotion or social media is clicked on.

Vanity metrics – Simple measurements that give an optimistic measurement in a restricted context, but do not accurately reflect the key drivers of marketing or business objectives.